by the same author

SHERRY
THE WINES OF EUROPE
(*published by Faber and Faber*)

Little Dictionary of Drink

Little Dictionary of Drink

JULIAN JEFFS

Pelham Books

First published in Great Britain by PELHAM BOOKS LTD
52 Bedford Square, London WC1B 3EF
1973

This edition by arrangement with Pelham Books Ltd 1974

Printed in Great Britain by
Hollen Street Press Ltd at Slough, Berkshire
and bound by Dorstel Press at Harlow, Essex

Introduction

This is a dictionary not an encyclopaedia; a little dictionary, not a standard one. Much of it first appeared in serial form in *Vogue* and was aimed at giving the answers to the more probable questions that people may want to ask when they come across a new word that they are not familiar with. It does not purport to treat its subject in depth nor is any entry more than an outline; it aims at being useful rather than comprehensive. For greater detail, specialist works should be consulted.

ABBOCCATO   Italian word used to signify a slightly sweet wine.

ABOCADO   The Spanish term corresponding to the Italian abboccato.

ABSINTHE   The name is derived from *absinthium* – wormwood, which is the principal flavouring, together with aniseed and many herbs, used in this very strong light green spirit. Invented in Switzerland quite early in the eighteenth century it was taken up by the French army a hundred years later and by the end of the nineteenth century it had become synonymous with bohemian vice in Paris. Said to have devastating effects on the nerves, its manufacture is now forbidden in both those countries though some is still made in Spain. Of avilable drinks, the nearest substitute is Pernod. Like absinthe, this becomes dramatically cloudy when water is added to it. The real devotee drips iced water into it slowly through a perforated spoon containing a lump of sugar.

A.C.   See APPELLATION CONTRÔLÉE.

ADVOCAAT   A bright yellow liqueur, originally Dutch but now made in other countries out of egg, brandy and other flavourings. It is very viscous and nourishing.

AFRICA   See NORTH AFRICA and SOUTH AFRICA.

AGUARDIENTE   A general term applied to a distilled spirit in a Spanish or Portuguese speaking country.

AHR   See GERMANY, THE LESSER KNOWN WINES.

ALE   See BEER.

7

ALELLA   See SPANISH TABLE WINES.

ALGERIA   See NORTH AFRICA.

ALOXE-CORTON   See BURGUNDY.

ALSACE   This delightful area of France, with its unspoilt ancient towns and its beautiful landscape beneath the Vosges mountains, has changed nationality between France and Germany as a politician's pawn. Both languages are spoken there and, so far as the wines are concerned, it is a good thing that Alsace is now once more firmly part of France; for when it was German its wines were overshadowed by the great growths of the Rhine, and the growers were reduced to the mass production of *ordinaires* and wines used for blending. Now they are concentrating on quality, and they grow some of the best dry white wines that are to be had.

It is very rare for an alsatian to be sold by the name of a vineyard, and when a leading shipper does sell such a wine it is likely to be exceptionally interesting. Vineyards are generally quite small and the wines are blended – and are none the worse for that: see BLENDING.

There are two things principally to look for on the label: the name of the shipper and the variety of grape. The former determines the quality and the latter the style, though shippers often supply a given style in various different qualities, distinguishing their best blends by phrases such as 'Reserve Exceptionelle'. German wine terms are also sometimes used (which *see*) The vintage generally matters less than with German wines. There is no point in laying down alsatians: they reach their best after a couple of years or so and tend to go off after six or seven.

Of the various grape varieties, that which shows most gloriously in Alsace is the Traminer. Wines that are specially fragrant are labelled as Gewürtztraminer. These dry white wines have an outstanding flavour and a spicy bouquet, wines capable of standing up to the flavour of the richest shellfish. The Riesling also gives wines of very high quality, closer to the German in style. Another excellent variety is the Muscat; in Alsace (unlike most other regions) it yields a dry wine but one that nevertheless shows the characteristic muscatel flavour and bouquet. The Pinot Blanc and Tokay (Pinot Gris) varieties also give fresh, sound wines while the Sylvaner, although associated more with quantity than with quality, provides pleasant wines that are generally excellent value.

The robust character of Alsatian wines enables them to stand up to a great variety of foods. They are at their best with fish, hors d'oeuvres, white meats and mild cheeses. They should be served slightly chilled. Wines blended from several varieties are sold as ZWICKER or EDELZWICKER.

ALTO DOURO See PORT

AMERICAN WINES Europeans hardly look upon the U.S.A. as a wine growing country, but nevertheless it has a substantial production of wine and many of its wines are excellent, particularly those grown in California; though when a stranger tastes the Californian wines that are commercially available he is usually tantalised by his American friends saying 'But if only you could taste the ones we don't sell.' Those that are available in this country are good and sound but scarcely worth the price at which they have to be sold. A certain amount of rather ordinary wine is also grown in Canada, but it is not exported.

Of Californian wines, about two thirds of those sold are fortified and are vinified in imitation of port and sherry, though there is also some fortified muscatel and a cheap and nasty sweet wine sold as angelica, which is said to take its name from Los Angeles. These wines are not generally exported and should not be sought out by visitors to the United States.

In the last few years, however, growers have been concentrating more of their energies into producing high quality table wines, with notable results. The best areas for these are the North Coast counties, especially Sonoma, Napa, Santa Clara, San Benito and the Livermore Valley in Alameda. To the great credit of the growers, their best wines are now generally being marketed under the names of the grape varieties from which they are vinified, which is a far better and more honourable way of marketing than that which was common in the past, namely to usurp a European geographical name. A Californian Sauvnignon Blanc or a Pinot Noir can stand on its own merits, whereas if they were called respectively graves or red burgundy the name would invoke unfair comparisons. A certain amount of sparkling wine is also produced, some of it by the *méthode champenoise* (see CHAMPAGNE).

9

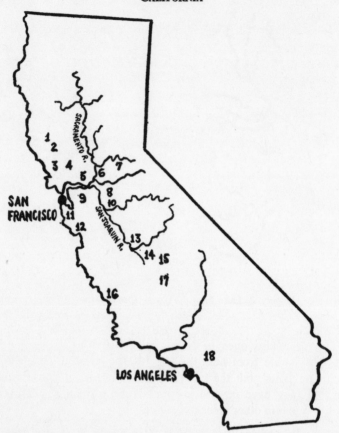

1 Ukiah. 2 Asti, Geyserville. 3 Healdsburgh, Guernville, Santa Rosa, St Helena. 4 Sonoma, Rutherford, Oakville, Napa. 5 Fairfield. 6 Elk Grove. 7 Plymouth. 8 Acampo, Lodi. 9 Livermore. 10 Ripon. 11 San Francisco, Saratoga, Los Gatos. 12 Felton, San Martin. 13 Madera. 14 Fresno. 15 Cutler. 16 Templeton. 17 Delano. 18 Guasti, Cucamonga, Etiwanda, Fontana.

Next after California the most important district is around the Finger Lakes in New York state. Fortified wines, table wines and sparkling wines are all grown there and until recently the sparkling wines enjoyed the best reputation, but now efforts are being made to improve the quality of the table wines and some are already available under varietal names.

10

NORTH AMERICA

1 Benton Harbor. 2 Lake Erie. 3 Lake Chautauqua. 4 Finger Lakes.

Ohio used also once to be an important wine growing area, and it was wine from near Cincinnatti that inspired Longfellow's 'Catanaba Wine', but the vineyards were eclipsed during Prohibition and they have never recovered. Vineyards on a small scale are also found in other areas (see map).

AMERICANO Originally a long cocktail made from one part of Campari to two of sweet Vermouth, iced and topped up with soda water. Now available ready bottled with only the soda water to be added.

AMONTILLADO See SHERRY.

AMOROSO See SHERRY.

AÑADA A Spanish term meaning a vintage wine.

ANGOSTURA A bitter flavouring made in Trinidad. Used in a number of cocktail recipes, and for making pink gin. To make this, a drop of Angostura is put in a glass and swirled round. The gin is then added.

ANIS Strong aniseed-flavoured aperitifs and liqueurs made in France and Spain. See LIQUEUR.

ANJOU See LOIRE.

APERITIFS An aperitif has two duties: to provide pleasure before dinner and to stimulate the appetite. The finest aperitifs will do both. The sweeter ones sometimes signally fail to achieve the latter.

To the British taste, there can be little doubt that the best aperitif of all is champagne. There is little point in serving a vintage champagne as an non-vintage will do equally well and may even be preferred before the meal. Next comes dry sherry or madeira. Still dry wines also make excellent aperitifs, especially on a hot summer's day. In France, especially in Burgundy, a popular drink is *vin blanc cassis* – a cheap, well-chilled white wine with a little of the local blackcurrant syrup added. The French also, for some inscrutable reason, favour tawny port, and in Britain there is some vogue for white port. On the Continent generally, especially in Italy, a glass of vermouth is popular. Some people, especially if wine is not taken with the meal, prefer spirits, such as gin, or a cocktail. But all these things have their own entries.

The home of the proprietary aperitif is France, and most of those that are popular today come from there. There is a wide variety to choose from and amongst the most popular are those with a red wine base, such as Ambassadeur, Byrrh, Cap Corse, Dubonnet and St Raphael. Apart from wine, sweetening and fortification, most of these aperitifs include quinine and various herbs, the exact formula invariably being a 'family secret'. Even if the base is red wine – and obviously if it is white – these are best taken well iced, often 'on the rocks' (with lumps of ice in the glass), and many people think them improved by a squeeze of lemon.

Of the stronger aperitifs, Pernod has already been mentioned under Absinthe. Pastis is the generic term for these aniseed-based strong aperitifs which, like Pernod, go milky when diluted. Amer Picon is a form of orange bitters, generally taken diluted and sometimes with a little *cassis* to take the edge of the bitterness. Suze is another strong, bitter, yellow aperitif, said to derive its flavour from gentian root. And there are many others. These are definitely acquired tastes.

APPELLATION CONTRÔLÉE (A.C.) In France this term is applied to wines which, according to French wine law, are entitled to certain geographical names. The laws are complicated and by no means infallible. Apart from specifying the geographical area in which the wines can be grown, other matters covered include, for example, the vine species, the maximum number of vines planted per hectare, the method of vinification, the minimum alcoholic strength, and so forth. The quantity of wine that can be produced from a given area is also laid down, any excess being sold without the benefit of the *appelation contrôlée*, and this in itself leads to one form of abuse: for different casks of the same wine may be sold with or without *appellation*, the latter fetching a lower price. The British market has often benefited from receiving these wines, which were nevertheless of unquestionable authenticity. This loophole, however, is likely to be closed now Britain has entered the Common Market. The abuse commences when the French merchant has sold so much wine without the *appellation* that he has more certificates left than he has wine to sell. Then he can 'stretch' his wine by blending it with another from elsewhere, and when the government inspectors examine his books they find that the amount of wine sold with certificates of origin corresponds with the amount originally available.

In Britain the words *appellation contrôlée* on a label at present have no legal significance whatsoever – a fact that wine drinkers can only regret. What is more, our laxity opens the way for abuses such as that described above. Despite the wine laws, the geographical accuracy of the labels from some districts are far more suspect than those from others. Burgundy labels are amongst the most suspect.

One step down from *appellation contrôlée* are the wines sold labelled V.D.Q.S. – *Vin Delimité de Qualité Supérieure*. Technically the regulations are somewhat less stringent, but in practice these wines are often more authentic than the former, as they come from the lesser districts whose products are less worth falsifying.

Similar wine laws exist in the other principal wine growing countries and work with varying degrees of efficiency. Political efforts to bring about the unification of Europe will no doubt eventually bring a standardized wine law into being, but at present differences in opinion and in vinification techniques between the member countries have prevented this happening, though it is well on the way.

APPLEJACK   See CALVADOS.

APRÉMONT   See FRANCE, THE LESSER KNOWN WINES.

AQUAVIT   Otherwise spelt *akvavit*, it is derived from the Latin *aqua vitae*, water of life. It is the same word as *eau de vie*, in fact (which *see*) but it is differently used, and denotes a highly rectified spirit, distilled in the Scandanavian countries from grain or potatoes and sometimes flavoured with caraway seeds. It is frequently taken there, drunk neat and well chilled, as an aperitif or at the beginning of a meal, with hors d'oeuvres or smoked fish, and although more brutal than almost any cocktail it seems suited to a northern climate.

ARBOIS.   See FRANCE, THE LESSER KNOWN WINES

ARGENTINA   Argentina is by far the largest wine growing country of South America, and although in the past it ranked second to Chile in terms of quality, it is now bidding fair to oust Chile from that position. Wines of every possible style are grown there. The two largest wine growing provinces are Mendoza and San Juan, both bordering on Chile, to the east of the Andes. In these provinces, wine growing is by mass production, and the quality is, generally speaking, rather poor. The finest wines are grown in the more southerly province of Rio Negro. They are altogether lighter and more delicate. Argentinian wines have already started to be imported into Britain on a substantial scale, and are likely to come here in greater quantities in the future.

ARMAGNAC   See BRANDY.

AROMA   See BOUQUET.

AR(R)ACK   A white spirit originally distilled from rice in the Dutch Indies and India, but now more generally used to indicate any sort of fiery native spirit.

ARROPE   Arrope has two meanings. In the sherry area, it is a

Arrope

SOUTH AMERICA

1 Valle del Cauca. 2 Lima. 3 La Paz. 4 Ica, Moquegua, Tacna. 5 Tarapaca.
6 Antofagasta, Catamarca. 7 Atacama. 8 Coquimbo. 9 Aconcangua,
Valparaiso, Santiago, O'Higgins, Colchagua, Curico. 10 Talca, Maule,
Linares, Nuble, Concepcion, Bio-Bio. 11 Salta. 12 Santiago del Estero.
13 La Rioja. 14 Cordoba. 15 Santa Fe. 16 San Juan, San Luis, Mendoza.
17 La Pampa. 18 Buenos Aires. 19 Neuquen. 20 Rio Negro. 21 Minas
Gerais. 22 Sao Paulo. 23 Parana. 24 Santa Catarina. 25 Misiones, Rio
Grande do Sur. 26 Soriana, San Jose, Canelones.

syrup made by boiling down must, and is used for sweetening brown sherries. In other parts of Spain, young grapes are boiled to the extent of producing a sort of jam, also known as arrope. It is excellent eaten with cheese.

ASTI SPUMANTE   See ITALIAN WINES.

AUDIT ALE   Originally a strong ale brewed in certain Oxford and Cambridge colleges to be drunk on audit day. That of All Souls' College Oxford was particularly famous. Nowadays these ales are brewed and sold commercially by the breweries, though some colleges still have special ales brewed for them. See BEER.

AUSTRALIA

1 Dardanup. 2 Gosnells. 3 Swan. 4 Clare, Barossa. 5 Langhorne Creek. 6 Berri. 7 Mildura. 8 Swan Hill. 9 Tahbilk. 10 Rutherglen. 11 Albury. 12 Bamswartha. 13 Coonawarra. 14 Great Weston. 15 Hunter River. 16 Roma.

AUSTRALIAN WINES   Wine growing in Australia can be traced back as far as the late eighteenth century, but although that is a long time in terms of the generations of man, it is little or nothing when compared with the antiquity of European vineyards. In 1831 a young settler by the name of James Busby returned to Europe and collected cuttings from 600 varieties of vine in order to find out which would be the best in the Australian soil and climate. But it takes a long time and much experiment before great wines are produced and the Australian wine industry, important though it is, may still be regarded as being in the experimental stage; the best wines of the future may well come from areas where the vine is not grown today.

In order of commercial importance the wine-growing states are: South Australia, notably in the Coonawarra, Langhorne Creek, Clare district, and Barossa valley; New South Wales, which includes the Hunter River area; Victoria, which includes the Great Western and Tahbilk areas; Western Australia; and Queensland. For general positions of these and other districts, see map.

Until recently the domestic market in Australia lacked connoisseurs, and production was concentrated on fortified wines of port and sherry styles, which inevitably suffered by comparison with their European prototypes, though some of the so-called 'sherries' are now quite good wines. The market for good quality table wines is steadily increasing and some excellent examples are to be had in this country at reasonable prices despite the freight charges.

AUSTRIAN WINES Steadily more Austrian wines are being imported, and very good they are. Their style is their own though they are comparable with German wines, especially with those from Baden, being fairly light and fresh, though somewhat less delicate; but there are no Austrian wines with anything like the finesse of the finest German ones. The white wines are generally better than the reds, and are much more widely grown. The vineyards are in Lower Austria, Burgenland, Styria and (to a very small extent) in the area of Vienna. Of these, Lower Austria is the most important and is itself divided into seven districts: Weinviertel, Wachau, Krems, Langenlois, Donauland, Baden, and Bad Vöslau. There are two basic classifications: splitzenweine and tischweine, being . respectively quality wines and ordinary table wines, though the former term is rather optimistically used. Apart from these, the normal German wine terms (which *see*) are used on the labels, though with some variations, such as *naturbelassen* to denote an unsugared wine and *gerebelt* to denote

17

a wine made from selected bunches of grapes. Austrian wines tend to mature quickly and are best when fresh and young.

AUXERRE See FRANCE, THE LESSER KNOWN WINES.

AYL See MOSELLE.

BADEN See GERMANY, THE LESSER KNOWN WINES.

BANDOL See FRANCE, THE LESSER KNOWN WINES.

BARBERA See ITALIAN WINES.

BARBARESCO See ITALIAN WINES.

BARDOLINO See ITALIAN WINES.

BARLEY WINE See BEER.

BAROLO See ITALIAN WINES.

BARSAC See BORDEAUX, WHITE.

BASTARD (RED OR WHITE) Sweet Portuguese wine vinified from the Bastardo grape.

BÂTARD-MONTRACHET See BURGUNDY.

BEAUJOLAIS See BURGUNDY.

BEAUNE See BURGUNDY.

BEAUMES-DE-VEISE See RHÔNE.

BEER One of the oldest fermented drinks, beer was well known to the ancient Egyptians. Some authorities indeed say that it pre-dates wine, despite the fact that it is far more complicated to make. In Britain, where practically all our wine has to be imported, beer can properly claim to be our national drink. We brew it well, too; it is a pity we do not make more fuss about it. As it is, the general quality is excellent but the absence of connoisseurs, or their diversion to wine drinking, has led to a shortage of brews worthy of connoisseurs; but many brewers have special beers that are worth looking for.

The process of brewing beer is complicated, but what happens, in a nutshell, is as follows. The raw material, barley, is first malted. The malting process consists first in soaking the barley so that it can absorb moisture. Then it is drained off and the corn starts germinating, so that small roots appear at the base. In the course of this germination the cellulose in the grain is converted into soluble starches. At the appropriate moment – and the malting has to be very carefully controlled – the process is arrested by increasing the temperature and the malt is then kiln dried. The method of drying – whether it is over a wood fire or in a cylinder, for example – makes a great difference to the style of the beer that is eventually brewed, and it accordingly has to be carefully selected and controlled.

After a period of storage, the malt is then mashed. It is first cracked in a mill to allow the liquor to penetrate the grains. The brewer then prepares a mixture of malts and other things such as sugar or maize flakes to give a brew of the style required. This mixture is put into a mash-tun with warm liquor (water). The importance of the particular water used is well known. Nowadays it is easy to adjust the composition of water to give what ever style of beer is required, but in the past, the great breweries have always been in towns such as Dublin, London, Burton-on-Trent and Stone, where the waters have been particularly suitable. During the mashing the soluble starches are converted into sugars and the liquor extracts the goodness to produce a liquid known as wort. Further extractions can then be made, each being weaker than the last. In olden days the third extraction was kept apart and fermented to make 'small beer'. Now it is generally used as the first liquor for a fresh extraction. An alternative method of mashing, used for making lager beer, starts with a cooler liquor but heats it in the mash-tun.

The next process is hopping, when the wort is boiled with hops in coppers. The traditional English 'ale' contained no hops – an innovation introduced in the fifteenth century, which led to the modern 'beer'. But now the two terms are used loosely and interchangeably. Next comes the fermentation. The wort is chilled and passed into fermenting vats in which the sugars, with the aid of yeast, are converted into alcohol. Different types of yeast are used depending on whether an ordinary or a lager beer is required. There are also, of course, important differences between the way in which the fermentation is carried out as between one brewery and another. After fermentation the beer is allowed to settle and is clarified before being put into barrels. Most bottled beers are fully fermented before bottling but some are allowed to complete their final fermentation in the bottle, notably Guinness and some kinds of Bass and Worthington.

The brewer is a very highly skilled man, and it follows even from the brief description of brewing given above that innumerable variations are possible, giving an infinitely wide choice of beers. Beer drinking habits also vary considerably in different areas; in the Black Country, for instance, many bars serve draught mild but no bitter, whilst in London the opposite is true.

Beers can conveniently be divided into four basic types: dark, light, strong, and lager. Of the dark beers, the darkest are the stouts. Guinness is perhaps the most famous of all, with plenty of hops and a bitter after-taste, in contrast with the London stouts which are generally sweeter. Then come the brown ales, and finally, lightest of the dark beers, come mild and Scotch ale.

The light beers include the various bitters, India pale ale, and so on. There are many justly famous brands. Nowadays there is a fashion for particularly light brews of the Keg type, which are certainly less soporific at lunch time.

The strong ales are a complete contrast. These are often sold in small bottles and have such a strong flavour that they come as quite a shock to the seasoned beer drinker when tried for the first time. Bass's No. 1 *Barley Wine* is such a brew. Somewhat darker strong beers include the famous Audit Ales, which take their name from the old custom of landowners to hold a feast with specially brewed beer on the audit day, when rent was due for payment. Good examples are still to be found in the Oxford and Cambridge colleges. The college beer at All Souls', Oxford, is especially fine and strong.

Finally, in complete contrast, come the lagers. These were originally associated with the Continent, the most famous being those of Denmark, Czechoslovakia, Germany and Alsace. More lager is now being brewed in the British Isles, and some of it is very good.

Finally a word about serving. First of all the beer must be in good condition. Draught mild, for instance, goes off very quickly, while some of the strong beers mature well in bottle. Generally speaking, though, it is wise to buy for quick consumption. If they are to taste at their best, light beers and lagers *must* be chilled: cellar temperature is admirable. Dark beers, and the darker strong beers, on the other hand, taste best at room temperature. As for the choice of food, as compared with wine, beer calls for less subtlety in arranging the partnership. On a hot day, cold draught bitter tastes well with almost anything and is especially happy with English roasts and grills. Guinness, on the other hand, is famous as a perfect partner for oysters.

BELLET See FRANCE, THE LESSER KNOWN WINES.

BÉNÉDICTINE See LIQUEURS.

BENICARLO See SPANISH TABLE WINES.

BERGERAC See FRANCE, THE LESSER KNOWN WINES.

BERNKASTEL See MOSELLE.

BIANCO Italian for white.

BISHOP See MULLED DRINKS.

BITTERS Spirits flavoured with various herbs, roots, etc., which give them a bitter taste, making them useful in preparing various cocktails. The best known include amer picon (France), angostura (which *see*), campari (Italy), fernet branca (Italy), and various forms of bitters made in Britain, such as orange bitters and peach bitters.

BLACK VELVET A mixture of approximately equal parts of champagne and stout. It is favoured as a drink to be taken with oysters.

BLANC-DE-BLANCS White wine made of white grapes in contrast to Blanc-de-Rouges which is white wine made of black grapes – a rare exception of which champagne is the outstanding example.

BLANQUETTE DE LIMOUX See FRANCE, THE LESSER Known WINES.

BLAYAIS See CLARET.

BLENDING For some inscrutable reason many would-be connoisseurs of wine profess to be horrified when ever the word blending is mentioned. This can only be regarded as one of their more absurd affectations. Some of the great wines are invariably blended – champagne, sherry, and port, for example. Wines sold under district names are also blended; for instance a wine sold

21

as *beaune* is (or should be) blended from wines grown in the various vineyards around the old town of Beaune in the Côte d'Or. Perhaps the ignominy which surrounds the conception of blending is partly derived from the fact that the geographical exactitude of these district names has become so suspect. Although the greatest wines from some districts are single vineyard wines, this does not apply to all the greatest wines – to the three previously mentioned, for example. Nor does it apply to the many excellent branded wines, for example the various brands of *liebfraumilch*. And in the future it is more than likely that some of the perfectly good wines at the moment masquerading under bogus district names will be more honourably sold under made-up names that have no geographical connotation. Blending is in fact an admirable process. The blender can choose a wine that is too sweet and blend it with another that is not sweet enough, a wine that is too acid with a wine that is lacking in acidity, and so on. If skilfully prepared, the resultant blend can then be more attractive than any of its constituents. Blended wines never attain the greatest peaks which single vineyard wines can achieve, but neither do they sink to the abysmal depths that a fine vineyard can be reduced to in a bad year.

BODEGA   A Spanish wine cellar, usually above ground.

BOMMES   See BORDEAUX, WHITE.

BOND   A store under Customs and Excise supervision where dutiable goods are kept prior to the duty being paid.

BONNES-MARES   One of the best red burgundies, grown in the communes of Chambolle-Musigny and Morey-Saint-Denis in the Côte de Nuits. See BURGUNDY.

BORDEAUX, RED   See CLARET.

BORDEAUX, WHITE. To many wine drinkers, white bordeaux means one of two things: graves or sauternes. But there are many more districts, and other wines exist in a bewildering variety, from the immensity and glory of Château d'Yquem to the humble little wines of Entre-Deux-Mers, from the luscious sweetness of a great vintage sauternes to the dry austerity of a white médoc. While connoisseurs honour the great dessert wines of sauternes and barsac with lip service, they seldom buy them, so that (with the exception of Château d'Yquem) the prices are startlingly low compared with wines of similar quality from other districts, and they often dismiss the drier wines altogether, which is unjust, as many are good even though none is great.

BORDEAUX

1 Médoc. 2 Haut-Médoc. 3 Graves. 4 Cérons, Barsac. 5 Sauternes. 6 Bordeaux St Macair. 7 Ste-Croix-du-Mont. 8 Loupiac. 9 Premières Côtes de Bordeaux. 10 Entre-Deux-Mêrs. 11 Graves de Vayres. 12 Côtes de Blaye. 13 Côtes de Bourg. 14 A.C. Bordeaux. 15 Fronsâc. 16 Pomerol, Lalande de Pomerol, Neac. 17 St Emilion. 18 Ste-Foy-Bordeaux.

White wines are grown in the following districts: Graves; Sauternes (which is surrounded on three sides by Graves, and which comprises the five communes of Sauternes, Bommes, Preignac, Fargues, and Barsac); Cérons (which is adjacent to Sauternes and also within Graves); the Médoc; St Emilion; Bourgeais and Blayais; Entre-Deux-Mers; Bordeaux Sainte-Foy (forming an extension of Entre-Deux-Mers to the north-east); Graves de Vayres (which is to the north of Entre-Deux-Mers, and surrounded by it, just as Sauternes is surrounded by Graves); the Premières Côtes de Bordeaux (which is a strip taken out of the south-west of Entre-Deux-Mers); Sainte-Macaire (which adjoins the south-eastern end of the Premières Côtes); Loupiac and Sainte-Croix-du-Mont (which are adjacent and which are in turn surrounded by the Premières Côtes de Bordeaux). It is all terribly confusing until one looks at the map; then it will be clear that the first named areas are broadly south-west of the Gironde; the next to the north-east; and those last named lie between the rivers Garonne and Dordogne. Since one must mention them in some sort of order, this seems as good as any; but it is less than satisfactory. The rivers form convenient geographical boundaries, and they obviously determine the lie of the slopes; but they do not necessarily coincide with the divisions in the soil. Looking at the map again, it will be seen that Loupiac and Sainte-Croix-du-Mont on the right bank of the Garonne face Cérons and Sauternes on the left bank. Geographically it would be just as logical to draw a circle around them and discuss them as a single area.

Graves grows some of the most popular white wines. Many are dry but most have a touch of sweetness and some are quite sweet. The dry wines are the most attractive: slightly chilled, they make good aperitifs, and they go well with fish. Although none is truly great, many are certainly good, and even the humblest of the dry wines are free from that unpleasant astringent acidity that sometimes spoils similar wines grown in other places. An outstanding but rare wine of this district is white Château Haut-Brion. Other excellent wines are grown in the following châteaux, which were classified in 1959:

Château Bouscaut	Cadaujac
Château Carbonnieux	Léognan
Château Chevalier	
(Domaine de Chevalier)	Léognan

Château Couhins	Villenave d'Ornon
Château Latour-Martillac	Martillac
Château Laville-Haut-Brion	Pessac
Château Malartic Lagravière	Léognan
Château Olivier	Léognan

The greatest of all the white bordeaux are grown in Sauternes – an enclave of specially good earth towards the south of Graves. It is rather flat and sun-drenched, so that here the grapes attain their greatest possible ripeness; indeed they go beyond ripeness and are affected by *pourriture noble* – literally 'noble rot' – which shrivels them to a raisin-like sweetness. But the sweetness of the wine is balanced by an intense flavour with great fruitiness.

The district of Sauternes includes four other communes one of which – Barsac – is almost as well known as Sauternes itself, and its wines can be sold under either name. This is the official classification, dating from 1855, which also gives the communes:

1st Great Growth

Château d'Yquem	Sauternes

1st Growths

Château Climens	Barsac
Château Coutet	Barsac
Château Guiraud	Sauternes
Château La Tour-Blanche	Bommes
Château Peyraguey	Bommes
Château Rabaud-Sigalas	Bommes
Château Rayne-Vigneau	Bommes
Château Rieussec	Fargues
Château Suduirant	Preignac

2nd Growths

Château Arche	Sauternes
Château Arche-Lafaurie	Sauternes
Château Broustet	Barsac
Château Caillou	Barsac
Château Doisy-Daene	Barsac
Château Doisy-Dubroca	Barsac
Château Doisy-Vedrines	Barsac
Château Filhot	Sauternes
Château Lamothe-Bergey	Sauternes

Château Lamothe-Espagnet	Sauternes
Château de Malle	Preignac
Château Myrat	Barsac
Château Nairac	Barsac
Château Romer-Lafon	Fargues
Château Suau	Barsac

Apart from their great sweet wines some of these châteaux also produce fairly dry wines. The dry wine of Yquem is sold as Ygrec and another excellent dry wine is grown by Château Filhot.

All the other districts listed earlier in this article grow white wines, and each has its characteristic style. Those grown in the Médoc, for instance, are dry, while those from Ste Croix-du-Mont are generally sweet, while Entre-Deux-Mers (it is actually between the two rivers and not between two seas) grows popular cheap wines of medium sweetness. To discuss each of these many districts in detail, however, is beyond the scope of this Little Dictionary.

BOTRYTIS CINEREA See 'NOBLE ROT'.

BOTTLES In ancient times wine was stored in leathern bottles or in containers made of skins sewn together. Such containers can still be seen in museums. The Greeks and Romans, on the other hand, had airtight *amphorae* which enabled the wine to mature over long periods so that vintage wine of some age is referred to in classical writings. The modern idea, however, of storing wine in glass bottles and fitting an airtight cork did not become a common practice until the eighteenth century and, after the disappearance of the classical amphorae, it was not until then that well matured vintage wine once more became a possibility.

There is an enormous range of bottle shapes and sizes, many of the famous wine districts having bottles which they regard as their own. The bordeaux bottle, for instance, has clearly defined shoulders, while the burgundy bottle tapers gradually towards the top, the champagne bottle being of a similar shape but made of thicker glass to withstand the high pressure. The bottles used for German and Alsatian wines are longer and more tapering, those for moselle and alsace being green while those for hock are

26

brown. Franconian wines are bottled in *bocksbeutels* – squat green flagons of a very attractive shape. Some bottles have pronounced punts: sections of the bottom that are pushed in to form a conical shaped dent inside the bottle. This is not done simply to make the bottle look larger than in fact it is, but it has the practical advantage that when the bottle is standing upright the sediment can sink down to the narrow part of the bottom which makes it easier to decant the wine while losing the minimum possible quantity.

The standard size of wine bottle in England, as used for most wines, is the 'reputed quart' containing twenty-six and two thirds fluid ounces, so that there are six reputed quarts to the gallon as compared with four imperial quarts. Larger bottles come in the following sizes:

	bottles
Magnum	2
Jeroboam or double magnum	4
Rehoboam	6
Methuselah	8
Salmanazar	12
Balthazar	16
Nebuchadnezzar	20

Apart from the magnum, however, these bottle sizes are seldom come across. It is generally agreed that the magnum is the best size of all for maturing wine over long periods. The larger bottle sizes tend to suffer from corking difficulties, while the smaller sizes enable the wine to mature more quickly, but somewhat less well. Apart from the advantage of half bottles on account of their size, they are useful in that they give one an early indication of how the wine is likely to develop in larger containers.

In Britain one is somewhat at the mercy of one's wine merchant, as there is no legal definition of bottle size, and the contents do vary somewhat as between one wine merchant and another. Little would be gained, however, by labelling the wine with the original contents, as most bottles tend to become ullaged, at least to a slight extent, with time, and so any labelling could be unintentionally misleading. Good wine merchants do not use bottles of sub-standard size, and that is the real protection. In

France the law is stricter and bottle sizes are clearly laid down.

	Centilitres
Litre	100
Champagne	80
Burgundy	80
Bordeaux	75
Anjou	75
Alsace	72

The litre size used seldom to be found in Britain, save in connection with vermouths and with some wines that are imported in bottle from the Continent, but it is now becoming more popular, especially with cheap wines. Chianti is commonly sold in litre flasks and, in assessing the cost of such a wine, a slide rule is a handy thing to have in one's pocket, so that the calculation can be made in terms of bottle size. It should be noted that Alsatian (and German) bottles are slightly smaller than the rest.

Finally, on the whole, beware of odd shaped bottles. If a wine is good, it will normally be bottled in something quite conventional, though appropriate to the district in which it originates. Occasionally one does find a good wine in a strange bottle, but it is always a source of surprise. The exceptions are sherry and port, where many of the most famous and most reputable shippers have decided for commercial reasons to adopt bottle shapes of their own devising. These contain a full measure of wine.

BOTTLE SCREW The eighteenth century term for a corkscrew.

BOTTLE SICKNESS A kind of malady which some red wines go through shortly after being bottled. The only cure is time and it generally goes away after about six months.

BOTTLE STINK An unpleasant smell that sometimes appears when wines are uncorked. It goes away with time.

BOUQUET The aroma of wine – one of the essential aspects of enjoying wine. It is for this reason that sensible glasses must be used, leaving an enclosed air space above the surface, so that the bouquet can collect. Sometimes the wine has to breathe for a certain period before the bouquet becomes evident, and it also tends to be subdued if the wine is too cold. Some tasters differentiate between the first impression given to the nose, and the over all effect on the nose, referring to the former of the bouquet and the latter of the aroma.

BOURBON This American whiskey takes its name from Bourbon county in Kentucky where it is said to have originated. There is a legal requirement that it should be made from not less than 51 per cent maize. The best brands are well matured in the wood, and are very high quality spirits by any standards.

BOURG, CÔTES DE BOURG See CLARET – BOURGEAIS.

BOURGOGNE ALIGOTÉ A not particularly distinguished white wine vinified in Burgundy from the Aligoté grape.

BOURGUEIL See LOIRE.

BRANDY This is not a geographical name. It can be made anywhere where wine is made, and it is. But to most brandy drinkers, the word is synonymous with cognac, an area in the Charente, to the north of the Gironde, which grows thin, acid and nasty white wines which distill to make exquisite brandy, far better than any that can be distilled from more attractive wines. It is in fact distilled three times in a pot still. Brandy must be aged in oak casks for at least five years before it becomes fit to drink and then, if it is to be sold commercially, it is blended by expert tasters who select spirits of varying ages and from different areas around Cognac which combine together to give a product of consistent quality. A certain amount of caramel is usually added, the amount varying, being less for good brandies than for cheap ones and more for some countries than for others. Some shippers are said also to add a touch of vanilla to some of their cheaper blends.

Confusion is sometimes caused by the phrase 'grande champagne'. It has nothing whatsoever to do with the wine champagne but is the name of the best district in which cognac is grown, followed by Petite Champagne, Fins Bois and others. Sometimes young vintage cognacs from a single district are shipped over to this country and are allowed to mature in cask, evaporating slightly year by year until they are bottled after twenty or more years in bond. To the taste of British brandy drinkers the result seems perfect, the brandy being the most subtle and delicate imaginable, but the French prefer the style of their own brandies, where the cask is refreshed from time to time, a little younger brandy being added.

A conventional series of abbreviations are used to indicate age, the youngest brandy normally exported being 3 star, followed by V.O. (very old), V.S.O. (very superior old), V.S.O.P.(very superior old pale) and X.O. (extra old), in order of age; but as standards differ from shipper to shipper it would be unwise to couple them with any particular number of years. In addition to these, various shippers have nomenclatures of their own, often giving fancy names to their finest brandies.

Armagnac, further to the south and approaching the Pyrenees, produces brandies that are less commercialised and less well known. Some frankly are fire water, but the best of them, although quite different in character from cognac, are equal to fine cognacs in maturity and quality. Many other parts of France produce acceptable brandies sold as 'grape brandy'.

Of the other brandies, some of the best are made in Spain, particularly by some of the sherry shippers. These brandies are not, however, distilled from sherry but from the weaker wines of La Mancha, being subsequently matured in the sherry towns by means of the solera system (which *see*). The best are excellent, but too many are doctored with cheap sweet sherry and other flavourings.

BRITISH WINES In the middle ages there were many vineyards in England, but our uncertain climate made wine growing a rather hazardous venture and since the suppression of the monasteries production has been very small. However the development, particularly in Germany, of new vines that ripen more readily in northern climates, and a fuller understanding of enology that enables pleasant wines to be vinified in years where sunshine is lacking, have combined to create a new interest, and wine growing is rapidly expanding here, with commercial vineyards in several counties including Berkshire, Hampshire, Sussex and Somerset. Some very pleasing white and pink wines are produced.

The term 'British Wines' is generally understood to refer not to those wines that are actually grown in Britain, but to 'wines'

fermented in Britain from grapes grown elsewhere. In the nineteenth century, these were generally prepared out of raisins, but
it is customary today for the manufacturers to import concentrated, unfermented grape juice (must) and to ferment it, with the
addition of various flavouring agents, in this country. The resultant alcoholic beverages are generally made to imitate port,
sherry, etc. They have the advantage of being attractive in price,
but are unlikely to appeal to serious wine drinkers.

BRUT   Indicates very dry, especially used of champagne.

BUAL   See MADEIRA.

BUCELLAS   See PORTUGUESE TABLE WINES.

BULGARIA   Although viticulture in Bulgaria is very ancient, it
was reorganised completely following the political upheaval, and
at present exports are mainly of cheap wines some of which are
vinified from the Riesling grape, which seems to have a local
flavour that distinguishes it from wines produced from it in
Germany, for instance. A sparkling wine made from this grape is
distinctly sweet and has a powerful flavour that is all its own. A
pleasant wine called misket is made from the red Muscat grape,
while the Melnik grape provides big, dark, heady red wines
which are often slightly sweet and have a curious, rather bitter
after-taste.

BULLS' BLOOD   See HUNGARIAN WINES.

BURGUNDY   The wines of Burgundy vie with those of Bordeaux in
their immense variety and they are often spoken of in the same
breath, for these are the two greatest table wine districts of
France and of the world. As might be expected there are certain
similarities between them and it is possible to pick wines from
the two districts – especially red wines – that would confuse experts in blind tastings. But the differences are far more marked
than the similarities. The red burgundies are fuller, rounder,
bigger, and smother than comparable clarets, while the white
burgundies are also bigger, drier, harder wines with a more
masculine appeal than the white wines of Bordeaux. Most
of them are completely dry and none has more than the
slightest trace of sweetness. Nearly all the vineyards are divided
into small holdings and there is a great deal of difference

BURGUNDY – LA COTE DE NUITS

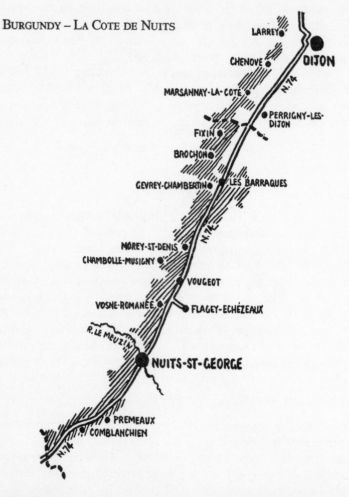

between the quality and style of the various growers. Most
burgundies are blended by the shippers from wines brought from
the growers and shippers tend to have distinct 'house styles'.
Since the wines are blended, and demand outstrips supply, there
is ample scope for 'stretching' by the less reputable. It is therefore best to buy burgundy off a good merchant whom
you can trust and to pay a fair price for it. For instance a
Nuits-St-Georges that reails under about a £1.30 (at the time of
going to press) may be regarded with suspicion and it is usually

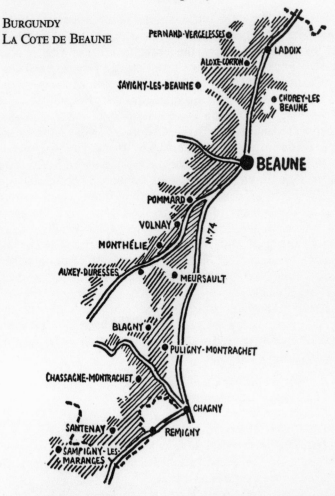

BURGUNDY
LA COTE DE BEAUNE

PERNAND-VERGELESSES

LADOIX

ALOXE-CORTON

SAVIGNY-LES-BEAUNE

CHOREY-LES-BEAUNE

BEAUNE

POMMARD

VOLNAY

N.74

MONTHÉLIE

AUXEY-DURESSES

MEURSAULT

BLAGNY

PULIGNY-MONTRACHET

CHASSAGNE-MONTRACHET

CHAGNY

SANTENAY

REMIGNY

SAMPIGNY-LES-MARANGES

worth while to pay more and to get a good one. If it has the name of a single vineyard on it, it will be a better bet still. Beware of bargains. People who boast of how cheaply they buy their burgundy are generally fools.

Burgundy is divided into three principal parts. In the north comes Chablis – an isolated island of fine vineyards with a very limited production of exquisite and distinctive white wines. (A name, by the way, that is much misused). Then comes the Côte d'Or – a golden slope of south to south-east facing vineyards, and this, as a glance at the maps will show, is itself divided into two parts: the Côte de Nuits in the north where the finest red wines and some good white wines are grown, and the Côte de Beaune in the south where the opposite is true. The famous communes of the Côte de Nuits (from north to south) are Fixin, Gevrey-Chambertin, Morey-St-Denis, Chambolle-Musigny, Vougeot, Flagey-Echézeaux, Vosne-Romanée, and Nuits-St-Georges, while those of the Côte de Beaune (also from north to south) are Pernand-Vergelesses, Aloxe-Corton, Savigny-les-Beaunes, Beaune, Pommard, Volnay, Monthélie Auxey-Duresses, Meursault, Blagny, Puligny-Montrachet, Chassagne-Montrachet and Santenay. Then further to the south, comes the Mâconnais and Beaujolais – areas of delicious but slighter wines which mature more quickly and many of which go down at a gulp. The most famous wines of the Mâconnais is the white Pouilly Fuissé (not to be confused with Pouilly Fumé from the Loire). The best known communes of Beaujolais are (from north to south) St Amour, Juliènas, Chénas, Moulin-à-Vent, Fleurie, Chiroubles, Morgon and Brouilly.

To classify the wines is complicated and quite beyond the scope of this dictionary, but an amateur of wine in 1888 drew up a family tree of the red wines and I cannot do better than to quote it, for it still holds good.

> *The Royal Family of the Wines of Burgundy*
> *The King:* le chambertin
> *The Queen:* la romanée-conti
> *The Regent:* le clos-vougeot
> *The King's first cousin:* le richebourg
> *Princes of the Blood:* romanée, clos-de-tart, musigny, la tâche, echézeaux, bonnes-mares.
> *Royal Standard Bearer:* le corton
> *Dukes and Duchesses:* volnay, nuits, pommard, beaune, savigny-vergelesses, aloxe-corton, chassagne.

The tree could much longer. A similar tree for white burgundies would undoubtedly begin with le montrachet followed closely by le chevalier montrachet and le bâtard montrachet then there would be chablis and meursault.

There is a difference of opinion as to the temperature at which red burgundy should be served. One thing is certain: it should never appear to be warm. The general view is that room temperature is best – but the temperature of the dining-room not of the kitchen. Another school of thought, however, favours cellar temperature and there can be no doubt that young beaujolais tastes very good when slightly chilled on a hot summer's day. White burgundies should always be slightly chilled. Being robust wines, burgundies tend to taste particularly good with flavoursome food. Coq au vin is a famous Burgundian dish, for instance. It can be made with wine of either colour and wine of a like colour drunk with it. The red wines are excellent with red meat, game, stews and dishes like ox-tail. The white wines are excellent as aperitifs (and so is a young chilled red beaujolais) or with fish dishes, veal and poultry. Beaujolais can be good in its first year – beaujolais de l'année, which is meant to be drunk within six months. Other burgundies are generally at their best between five and twelve years old. See also BONNES-MARES, CHAMBERTIN, CLOS DE VOUGEOT, HOSPICES DE BEAUNE, ROMANÉE-CONTI, VINTAGE.

CABINET   See GERMAN WINE TERMS.

CAHORS   See FRANCE, THE LESSER KNOWN WINES.

CALIFORNIA   See AMERICA.

CALVADOS   This is a spirit distilled from cider in the province of that name in Normandy. During the war, stocks of well matured spirit practically gave out and the young calvados which was later imported was fiery and strong but little else. Now well matured *vieux calvados* is available again and has the subtlety of a fine spirit, but it is something of an acquired taste. A similar spirit is known in America as *applejack*.

CAMPARI   An Italian proprietary aperitif; a red Vermouth flavoured with bitters. Generally taken iced with soda.

CANARY ISLANDS   In ancient times the Canary Isles were renowned for their 'Canary sack' – a sweet wine which was evidently of great distinction. The vineyards were virtually wiped out by disease in the nineteenth century, and although wine is now grown on a substantial scale, none of it has gained acceptance in export markets.

CANTENAC   See CLARET.

CAPRI   See ITALIAN WINES.

CARAFE   A flask used for serving wine, hence carafe wines which are generally relatively humble wines, often drawn straight from the wood and served in carafes in restaurants.

CARCAVELLOS   See PORTUGUESE TABLE WINE.

CARDINAL   See MULLED DRINKS.

CARIÑENA   See SPANISH TABLE WINES.

CASSIS   Has two distinct meanings. The first is a white wine grown in the south of France (see FRANCE, THE LESSER KNOWN WINES). The second is a blackcurrant syrup commonly drunk with white wine.

CASTELLI ROMANI   See ITALIAN WINES.

CECUBO   See ITALIAN WINES.

CELLARS   Cellars are the best places for keeping wine in, not through there being any magic in being underground, but simply because the temperature tends to remain more constant, see TEMPERATURE. Being underground they are normally free from vibration which disturbs maturing wine. It does not really matter if a cellar is damp or even if it gets flooded from time to time provided that it is flooded with pure water, the only snag is that it washes the labels off. This can be a grave disadvantage to members of the wine trade, but matters very little in a private cellar provided that a proper record is kept of the whereabouts of all the contents. An ideal temperature is about 50–55°F., which has the incidental advantage that white wine is at just the right temperature for drinking. Bottles of wine should be binned on their sides to keep the corks moist and vintage port should be binned with the dabs of whitewash uppermost so that the crust continues to settle in the same place as it did in the wine merchant's cellar. Metal and wood honeycomb bins are readily available and are as good as any. Spirits, on the other hand, should be kept upright, as a minute leakage of air does not do them any harm and they tend to eat away at their corks if left in contact with them for too long. Finally a lot of fun can be had by keeping a cellar book, listing all the wines stocked, with prices and comments. Such books make fascinating reading after the lapse of years.

CÉPAGE   Vine variety.

CÉRONS   See BORDEAUX, WHITE.

CHABLIS   See BURGUNDY.

CHAMBERTIN   One of the very finest red burgundies, but production is very limited so that the price for the genuine wine is necessarily high. The neighbouring vineyard of Clos de Bèze is also entitled to be sold as chambertin, but is generally sold as Chambertin Clos de Bèze. Other fine growths in the area are entitled to hyphenate their names with that of Chambertin. Although they are not quite the equal of Chambertin and Clos de Bèze, they come very close. They are:

> Charmes Chambertin
> Chapelle Chambertin
> Griotte Chambertin
> Latricières Chambertin
> Mazis Chambertin
> Mazoyères Chambertin
> Ruchottes Chambertin.

In contrast, Gevrey-Chambertin is simply the village name, and although excellent wines are sold under this more general appellation, they are not to be confused with those mentioned above. Also see BURGUNDY.

CHAMBÉRY   An ancient town in the Savoy where white wines are grown, but it is best known for its vermouth which is very dry, and of outstanding quality.

CHAMBOLLE MUSIGNY   See BURGUNDY.

CHAMBRER   To bring the wine up to the temperature of the room in which it is to be drunk. See TEMPERATURE.

CHAMPAGNE   There is nothing to compare with the sparkle of champagne: it is a metaphorical sparkle as well as a physical one. No other wine is so full of joy. It is the perfect wine for a party, and the supreme aperitif, especially in warm weather. It is wonderfully versatile, too, and tastes well with almost anything. But if it sounds too good to be true it must be admitted that its gaiety hides one danger: drink too much, and the hangover is terrible; moreover it brings with it an unquenchable thirst. The vineyards of Champagne are the most northerly of the great French vineyards, and only those of Germany lie further north in the whole of Europe. To grow wines in such a latitude is hazardous and difficult. It is only worth while owing to their exceptional grace, and to the high price that this enables them to command. But wine has been grown in Champagne ever since the days of the Roman occupation, and apart from introducing the vine, the Romans did another great work: they mined chalk, and their ancient workings provide the basis of the great cellars that lie two to three hundred feet deep beneath the city of Rheims. Those of Pommery and Greno alone extend for some ten miles.

In the early days the wines were not at all like those we know now; they were still, and many of them were red. In flavour they were rather like a lighter style of burgundy. We owe the modern, sparkling wine largely to the genius of Dom Pérignon, a monk who was appointed cellarer of the Benedictine Abbey of Hautvillers, near Epernay, in 1668. It was already well known that champagne tended to have a second fermentation, which gave it a slightly pétillant quality, something like that of the Portuguese *vinhos verdes* that are so popular today. It has often been claimed that Dom Pérignon 'put the bubbles in'; but that, of course is nonsense: they were already there. He did manage to keep them in, though, by tightly corking the bottles at the right moment, and he also made better wines, both still and sparkling, than had been known before. By the time he died in 1715 the sparkling wine was well established.

Nowadays champagne is made by the *méthode champenoise*. It is complicated and it takes a long time. It is therefore necessarily expensive. But it is worth it. After the must has fully fermented a blend is made by selecting wines from various areas and sometimes also from various vintages to give a cuvée of exactly the style that the shipper requires. This is bottled and a second fermentation is provoked by adding a syrup consisting of sugar dissolved in wine to which yeasts have been added. This brings about a second fermentation which evolves carbon dioxide: the gas that gives champagne its bubbles. It also produces a sediment that has to be very gently shaken down over a long period until it forms a compact disk next to the cork, the bottles being by then upside down. Then comes the dramatic *dégorge-*

ment. The neck of the bottle is frozen and the cork quickly removed, bringing the sediment with it. Finally comes the *dosage*, when the bottles are topped up with the wine in which a little sugar is dissolved to give the champagne its required degree of sweetness. It is then tightly corked and matured for a while before being sold.

It is not often realised that about sixty per cent of the wine that goes into a normal champagne is vinified from black grapes which are pressed so quickly that the skins are not in contact with the juice for long enough to impart any noticeable degree of coloration. If pink champagne is required (rather an affected wine), a little of the local still red wine is blended in. The most usual names under which champagne is sold, indicating the degree of sweetness, are, from sweetest to driest: *doux, demi-doux, demi-sec, sec* or *dry, extra dry, brut* or *nature*. The *sec* is generally the most popular kind, and it is a good compromise, going well with food of most kinds. For those with a dry palate, the drier kinds make particularly fine aperitifs while the sweeter kinds, which are met with more often on the Continent than in Britain, go admirably with the sweet course of a meal. Those who want a particularly light and delicate aperitif wine for a hot summer's day might choose a *blanc de blancs*: a champagne vinified wholly out of white grapes, which has become peculiarly fashionable owing to its having been favoured by the late Mr James Bond. Delightful in its way, it is, however, by no means the epicurean miracle that it is sometimes made out to be, and most people tire of it long before they tire of the normal kind. Next, in choosing a champagne, there is the vintage to consider. The general taste is for a wine of six to eight years old, but some prefer far older wines – at least ten years old – wines that have become gentle in bottle and have acquired a fascinating, deep bouquet. Non-vintage wines are often preferable to very young vintages and in any case are quite good enough for use as an aperitif. Anyone who serves a vintage champagne at a party must have more money than sense or taste. Finally, which shipper? All the famous ones make good wines, and which you prefer is an entirely personal matter. For a party you can often get a bargain by going to a good, reliable wine merchant and choosing the wine that he sells under his own private brand name.

Champagne should be served chilled but not frozen stiff: say at about 50°F. Above all it should be served in a tall, narrow glass, or failing that a normal kind of wine glass: never in one of those ghastly flat saucers, so favoured fifty years ago, which let the wine slop over and release all the bubbles, while presenting a wide surface over which the bouquet cannot gather.

CHAMPAGNE COCKTAIL See COCKTAIL.

CHAMPAGNE, FINE See BRANDY.

CHANTE-ALOUETTE See RHONE.

CHAPTALIZATION A process taking its name from the French chemist, Count Chaptal, who advocated the addition of sugar to grape juice prior to the fermentation in order to enhance the alcohol. Wines made by this process are never as good as those made without it, but on the other hand, when there has been insufficient sun to produce sweet grapes, it enables a drinkable wine to be made in a vintage where the wine would otherwise be altogether too weak and thin. Used properly, therefore, it does nothing but good; but unhappily it is often abused.

CHARTREUSE See LIQUEUR.

CHASSAGNE-MONTRACHET See BURGUNDY.

CHATEAU Usually translated as *castle* and one or two of them actually are castles – Château d'Issan in the Médoc, for instance, and Château Olivier in Graves – but most are not castles at all, and may vary from anything between the eighteenth century elegance of Châteaux Beychevelle and Langoa to the ninteenth century ugliness of Châteaux Cantenac-Brown or Lanessan. Indeed, the word *château* in the Bordeaux area has really come to mean nothing more or less than the name of a vineyard; for there is hardly a 'château' at Château Mouton Rothschild, and there is no building of any kind at all at Château Léoville-Barton. While the word is largely associated with Bordeaux, it is occasionally found in other wine growing districts. The term *château bottled* is used when the wine is put in bottles at the château. If *château bottled*, the origin of the wine is put beyond doubt, but the wine trade, at any rate in Britain, is so honest that there is really no doubt in practice if the wine is bottled here, and some British wine merchants seem to know a good deal more about bottling wines than some châteaux, where the bottling is done very casually in odd moments. However, more often than not, château bottlings taste somewhat better than British bottlings in blind tastings, perhaps because some châteaux keep the best back for this purpose, although others refrain from bottling any at the châteaux at all – Léoville Barton (until recently) and Pontet-Canet, for instance. Château bottled wine used to cost a great deal more than British bottled because of a differential rate of duty, but this has largely been abolished, any difference that there may be now resulting from increased freight and snob value. It must be admitted that château bottled wines usually fetch more in auction than British bottled.

CHÂTEAU-CHÂLON   See JURA.

CHÂTEAU GRILLET   See RHÔNE.

CHÂTEAUNEUF-DU-PAPE   See RHÔNE.

CHÉNAS   See BURGUNDY.

CHERRY BRANDY   See LIQUEUR.

CHEVALIER-MONTRACHET   See BURGUNDY.

CHIANTI   See ITALIAN WINES.

CHILE   Chile used to make the best wines in the South American continent, and there is no denying the fact that it still has the best potential, but recent reorganisations in the wine trade following a socialist triumph have resulted in an oenological disaster. The best wines are grown in the central zone, particularly in the general area of Santiago. Much red wine is vinified from cabernet grapes, and this is very good indeed, though its resemblance to the wines vinified from the same vines in Bordeaux is very slight indeed, with Chilean wines being much bigger, heavier and less subtle. So far the vineyards have remained free of the phylloxera.

CHINON   See LOIRE.

CHIROUBLES   See BURGUNDY.

CIDER   Like beer, cider is somewhat unjustly neglected by gastronomes – presumably because it is native produce. Nevertheless we drink twenty million gallons of it a year. In the West Country and in Hereford, farmhouse cider is the traditional drink, bearing the same sort of relationship to the commercial product as does home brewed beer to commercial beer. My own taste, both for cider and for beer, is unashamedly for the commercial product. Some of the home-made ciders are extremely strong, and some of them are no doubt very well made, but others tend to go acid and remind one of peasant wines as compared with the the fine wines of the great commercial growers. In these areas, too, there are pubs that sell cider exclusively, and some of them enjoy fine local reputations. Although cider making as a substantial industry dates back only to the last century, it owes its origin to the seventeenth century Viscount Scudmore, who produced a first class cider apple – Scudmore's Arab – and whose studies of cider making did much to improve the quality.

To produce commercial cider, the apples are first washed and then pulped, the pulp forming a 'cheese' which is then pressed and the juice fermented. The result is a still, dry cider, and such ciders are available commercially. But most ciders are sweetened and carbonated. Other than the English ciders, the best known are those of Normandy. It is strange that many people regard cider as a non-alcoholic drink. It is nothing of the sort, and commercial ciders are just as intoxicating as beer. Cider should always be served cool.

CINQUETERRE   See ITALIAN WINES.

CLARET   To an Englishman, the word claret signifies but one thing: the red wine of Bordeaux. Unlike many wine names, it cannot truly claim to be geographical, at least in origin, and like many other wine names it is widely misused. For instance one comes across such contradictions such as 'Spanish claret'. But real claret comes from Bordeaux just as real sherry comes from Spain, and claret drinkers claim that this is the most fascinating wine in the world. They will hear no argument, and they certainly have a case, for no other wine presents so many subtle distinctions and variations. Clarets, too, are amongst the most authentic of wines, and you can nearly always trust the label implicitly. For this reason it is relatively easy to study claret and to obtain a real knowledge of the various parts of Bordeaux.

Bordeaux, moreover, has a special place in the history of

wine drinking in this country, for the vineyards were once on English soil. In 1152, Eleanor, who was Duchess of Aquitaine in her own right, married Henry Plantaganet, Count of Anjou. When he succeeded to the throne of England, two years later, the whole of Bordeaux, Gascony and Guienne became English possessions, and Bordeaux was not lost until 1453. Many of the Bordelais are still of English descent, and ever since this distant time bordeaux – and particularly red bordeaux – has been preeminent amongst our table wines, despite a comparative eclipse during the eighteenth century when our politicians saw fit to discriminate against French wines in favour of those of Portugal.

Originally 'claret' indicated a fairly light red wine – darker than rosé but lighter than wines that we know today. Nowadays, however, the word applies to fine deep red wines, and to none other. These are grown in the Médoc, Graves, Premières Côtes de Bordeaux, Blayais and Bourgeais, Fronsac, Entre-Deux-Mers, Saint-Emilion, and Pomerol. Most of these areas are further divided into more exact *appellations*. The greatest wines come from the first two and the last two named.

The Médoc is the greatest of all these districts and is divided half way along into two parts: the southern end, where the best wines are grown, is called the Haut-Médoc, while the northern end is the Bas-Médoc – or just plain Médoc. Travelling north up the Haut-Médoc from Bordeaux, the various main districts are reached in the following order: Margaux (with Cantenac), Moulis, Listrac, Saint Julien, Pauillac, Saint Estèphe. It is in these areas that most of the very finest wines are to be found – particularly in the first and in the last three.

In England we do not always realise that the district of Graves grows far more red wine than white, and was synonymous with the red wines of Bordeaux before the rise of the Médoc early in the nineteenth century. As it is, when the red wines of Bordeaux came to be classified in 1855, one outstanding château from Graves was included amongst them: Château Haut Brion. The first growths are:

Château Lafite	Pauillac
Château Margaux	Margaux
Château Latour	Pauillac
Château Haut-Brion	Pessac

The first château in the second growths is Château Mouton-Rothschild, but to include it amongst the second growths is really rather an insult, as it is worthy of comparison with any of the first growths. So for the purpose of the following table it will be omitted. The other growths are, in alphabetical order:

Château		*Growth*
Batailley	Pauillac	5th
Belgrave	Saint-Laurent	5th
Beychevelle	Saint-Julien	4th
Boyd-Cantenac	Margaux	3rd
Branaire-Ducru	Saint-Julien	4th
Brane-Cantenac	Cantenac	2nd
Calon-Ségur	Saint-Estèphe	3rd
Camensac	Saint-Laurent	5th
Cantemerle	Macau	5th
Cantenac-Brown	Cantenac	3rd
Clerc-Milon	Pauillac	5th
Cos-d'Estournel	Saint-Estèphe	2nd
Cos-Labory	Saint-Estèphe	5th
Croizet-Bages	Pauillac	5th
Dauzac	Labarde	5th
Desmirail	Margaux	3rd
Ducru-Beaucaillou	Saint-Julien	2nd
Duhart-Milon	Pauillac	4th
Durfort-Vivens	Margaux	2nd
Ferrière	Margaux	3rd
Giscours	Labarde	3rd
Grand-Puy-Ducasse	Pauillac	5th
Grand-Puy-Lacoste	Pauillac	5th
Gruaud-Larose	Saint-Julien	2nd
Haut-Bages-Liberal	Pauillac	5th
Haut-Batailley	Pauillac	5th
Issan	Cantenac	3rd
Kirwan	Cantenac	3rd
Lagrange	Saint-Julien	3rd
La Lagune	Ludon	3rd
Langoa	Saint-Julien	3rd
Lascombes	Margaux	2nd
La Tour-Carnet	Saint-Laurent	4th

Château		*Growth*
Léoville-Barton	Saint-Julien	2nd
Léoville-Las-Cases	Saint-Julien	2nd
Léoville-Poyferré	Saint-Julien	2nd
Le Prieuré	Cantenac	4th
Le Tertre	Arsac	5th
Lynch-Bages	Pauillac	5th
Lynch-Moussas	Pauillac	5th
Malescot-Saint-Exupéry	Margaux	3rd
Marquis d'Alesme-Becker	Margaux	3rd
Marquis-de-Terme	Margaux	4th
Montrose	Saint-Estèphe	2nd
Mouton-d'Armailhacq	Pauillac	5th
Palmer	Cantenac	3rd
Pédesclaux	Pauillac	5th
Pichon-Longueville	Pauillac	2nd
Pichon-Longueville-Lalande	Pauillac	2nd
Pontet-Canet	Pauillac	5th
Poujet	Cantenac	4th
Rausan-Ségla	Margaux	2nd
Rauzan-Gassies	Margaux	2nd
Rochet	Saint-Estèphe	4th
Saint-Pierre-Bontemps	Saint-Julien	4th
Saint-Pierre-Sevaistre	Saint-Julien	4th
Talbot	Saint-Julien	4th

This 1855 classification would, were it to be made today, be rather different: some châteaux have gone up in quality and others down, while there are several which for various reasons were not included in the 1855 classification and which would undoubtedly be included in any re-classification today. That is why, in the above list, the 2nd, 3rd, 4th and 5th growths are not separated: if a wine is good enough to be included in the list at all, it is very good indeed. Perhaps the most surprising thing is the consistency of the wines over the last hundred years rather than the fact that some of them now warrant a different classification.

The red graves have a distinctive flavour that is all their own – Château Haut-Brion comes first, then Château La Mission Haut-

Brion comes a very close second, and several other châteaux are included in a recent classification.

The wines of Saint Emilion and Pomerol are particularly 'big': there is something of burgundy about them, especially about Pomerol, and indeed many an expert has been fooled in a blind tasting when someone has selected a big bodied wine from one of these communes and compared it with a lighter style of burgundy. There are many excellent wines in these areas and they have their own well informed following. If they are perhaps less well publicised and less well known than the famous châteaux of the Médoc, nevertheless the wines compare, especially in some years, with any that can be grown in Bordeaux. The two greatest châteaux of Saint Emilion are Cheval Blanc and Ausone while the greatest in Pomerol is Pétrus.

On the whole the clarets from these major districts take a considerable amount of time to mature, though the exact amount of time depends on the year. For example, 1960 clarets were excellent drinking in 1967, (though some of them will go on being excellent for a few years yet) and many 1961 wines are by no means ready even now. First quality wines of a very good vintage are not normally expected to be mature for about fifteen or twenty years; in lesser vintages they may take anything from seven years upwards. In view of the very considerable variations that exist between different vintages and between different châteaux of the same vintage, as regards the rate of development of the wine, one either has to take a gamble, or to taste the wines at intervals during their developments, or (and this is the only way open to most people) to ask the advice of a reliable wine merchant. It is worth taking a little trouble, for a well matured claret is an incomparable wine, whereas the greatest clarets, when only a year or two old, shrivel the tongue with tannin and acidity. On the whole, if you want to drink a claret young, buy a cheap wine, preferably from one of the lesser districts mentioned at the beginning, such as a Bourg, whereas if you go to the expense of buying a classified growth of a good year, then give it long enough in bottle to mature properly. An immature first growth will taste far worse than a humble Côtes de Fronsac of the same age.

CLASSIFICATIONS The French have a tidy passion for classification. In a guide book, one is alarmed to see cathedrals classified with a system of stars as if they were A.A. recommended hotels: it seems somewhat blasphemous. Even the famous chickens of Bresse are protected by an *appellation contrôlée,* and what can be done for fowl can obviously be done for wines. But wines are much more capricious than cathedrals. A gothic church will not change from one year to the next, save in its minor embellishments, but a wine of one vintage may differ radically from its predecessor; and over a period of years the whole character of a vineyard may change owing to altered viticulture. Moreover, because wine is so capricious in its development, anyone who attempts to classify vineyards with any sort of precision is trying to outwit nature, like a handicapper at a race. His efforts will always be foiled when a great vineyard proves disappointing or when a lesser growth produces an outstanding wine. Even so, a classification is valuable provided it is used intelligently. Since the quality of a wine depends ultimately on the soil and climate, it will be consistent if taken over a sufficient period of years. It is in the light of this that one must consider such classifications as that of the Médoc, reproduced under claret. The same thing applies to vintage charts. All these things are generalisations, and the exceptions are often more fascinating than the norm.

CLIMAT   A Burgundian term to indicate the geographical qualities of the vineyard.

CLOS-DE-TART   See BURGUNDY.

CLOS-DE-VOUGEOT   One of the largest vineyards of the Côte de Nuits, originally a church property. It is now unfortunately divided amongst many small proprietors, and the quality is therefore distinctly variable, but the finest wines are very good indeed. Inside it is the château de Vougeot, a magnificent renaissance castle containing a collection of old wine presses.

COASTER   A stand, traditionally with a wooden bottom backed with baize and a surround of silver or Sheffield plate, for holding a decanter to prevent it from dripping on the table. As its name suggests, it can be coasted over the surface of the table from one diner to another. Coasters have also been made in porcelain. Some old coasters are fitted with wheels.

COCKTAILS The origin of the word *cocktail* is wrapped in mystery, and the stories about it are legion, most of them too fantastic to be bothered with. When cocktails were wildly in fashion, in the 1920s, some of the smarter barmen tried to make a mystique about them, but that need not be bothered with, either. Conversely, wine drinkers tend to sneer at them. This may be nonsense or it may not: it depends on the wine and on the cocktail. A *dry martini* would certainly do no harm to a bottle of red rioja, but a *white lady* (delicious though it is) would be sheer disaster before a fifty-year-old claret. The delicate flavour of the wine would be utterly overwhelmed and lost.

The function of a cocktail is to be the herald of a meal, to whet the appetite for what is to come; so it should be short, cool and stimulating. Most cocktails have a basis of gin blended with vermouths, bitters, liqueurs, fruit juices and so on, but nowadays cocktails based on whisky, rum and vodka are getting more popular, while some people hold (reasonably, I think) that brandy-based cocktails are the best before wine.

Part of the bogus mystique concerned the way cocktails should be shaken or mixed. Some people always use a shaker, presumably because they like the sound of the ice in it, rattling about; but shakers are only really necessary when fruit juice is being used, as they then help to amalgamate the ingredients. Otherwise stir the mixture in a jug – but stir it well. Jugs with specially formed narrow lips are the best as they do not let the ice cubes fall into the glass. Use plenty of ice and never mix two kinds of cocktail with the same ice (And see ICE). Anyone prepared to face the research could probably find two or three thousand published recipes, and it would not call for too much ingenuity to think up as many more, but there are probably only twenty or thirty in common use.

The following are representative recipes for some of the most popular cocktails. Different books give different versions, and all can be modified to taste.

alaska: two thirds gin and one third yellow chartreuse, with or without a dash of orange bitters.

bloody mary: four parts tomato juice, three parts vodka, one part lemon juice and a good dash of Worcester sauce.

bronx: originally two parts orange juice and one part gin with a dash each of Italian and French vermouths, but the proportion of gin has crept up to half and sometimes the orange juice appears as only a sliver of peel.

champagne: a lump of sugar is put in a glass and very cold, cheap (it is to be hoped!) champagne is poured over it. A teaspoonful of brandy is sometimes added. It is completed with a small slice of orange or of lemon peel.

clover leaf: one part fresh lemon juice, two parts gin, one part grenadine, with the white of one egg, and a sprig of fresh mint on top.

daiquiri: one part fresh lime juice to three parts white rum with a teaspoonful of sugar per glass, a dash of maraschino (or not, according to taste) and a cherry on top if you fancy it. Must be well iced and served immediately after shaking.

maiden's blush: some versions include absinthe, but a safer and more practical recipe consists of a cocktail glass of gin with four dashes of curaçao, four dashes of grenadine, and one of fresh lemon juice.

manhattan: one part Italian vermouth to two parts rye whisky with a dash of angostura bitters.

martini: this is by far the most famous cocktail of all. A simple martini consists of half gin and half dry vermouth, but the public now favours *dry martinis*, consisting of two thirds gin, or even *very dry martinis*, going up to six sevenths gin: indeed some martinis nowadays seem only to have caught sight of the cork of the vermouth bottle and are little more than an excuse for swigging neat gin. A sweet martini is made from sweet Italian vermouth.

negroni: equal parts of gin, Italian vermouth and campari, garnished with orange rind.

old fashioned: one teaspoonful sugar with three dashes of angostura bitters, one part water and two of rye whisky garnished with a slice of orange peel, a twist of lemon and a cherry.

side car: equal parts of brandy, cointreau and fresh lemon juice.

white lady: as a side car but using gin instead of brandy. Some people like to increase the proportion of gin to a half. See also FIZZES.

COFFEE See IRISH COFFEE.

COGNAC See BRANDY.

COINTREAU See LIQUEUR.

COLARES   See PORTUGUESE TABLE WINES.

COLLINS   A long iced drink originating in the United States. Here is a recipe dating from 1895 for a Brandy Collins:

> Cut a lemon in half, place it in a mixing glass, add one tablespoonful of fine sugar, crush with muddler so as to extract both the juice of the lemon and part of the oil of the rind, fill the glass half full of fine ice, add one jigger [1½ oz.] brandy. Mix well, strain into a Collins-glass containing a piece of ice, pour in a bottle of plain soda. Stir with a long bar spoon and serve.

A John Collins is made in the same way, but using Dutch gin instead of brandy, a Tom Collins uses London Dry gin, and a Whisky Collins uses whisky.

COMMANDERIA   See CYPRUS.

CONDRIEU   See RHÔNE.

COSTANTIA   See SOUTH AFRICA.

COOKING   Many recipes are available using beer, cider various wines and even spirits. In cooking any dish using any of these, the alcohol evaporates before the wine and generally there is none left. There remain, however, various elements of flavour. Table wines, beer and cider tend to tenderise meat, and their flavour, although undoubtedly present, is not assertive, so that it would normally be impossible, in a meat dish cooked with wine, to say which wine it was cooked with. This, however, applies only to table wines. The fortified wines – sherry, madeira and marsala – have much more distinctive flavours which remain, usually clearly discernible, in the dishes in which they are incorporated. Very often cheap wine, or wine that is left over from a meal, is referred to as 'cooking wine', but the term is really an absurd one. If the flavour of a wine makes it not fit to drink, then it is not fit to cook with. On the other hand, good wines are so rare and expensive that to use them for cooking would generally be as absurd as it would be extravagant. Sound, cheap wines are usually best for this purpose.

CORDIAL   See LIQUEUR.

CORKED, CORKY   The latter term is more correct, as nearly all wines are 'corked' in a literal sense. A corky wine is one that has very disagreeable and distinctive odour and flavour derived from the use of a bad cork. The cork itself, when it is pulled out of the bottle, generally has this odour to a marked degree, and it is worth smelling the cork simply as a preliminary warning. Usually there is no visual sign that the cork is defective. If a bottle of wine is corky, there is only one thing to do with it: pour it down the drain. Fortunately very few are so infected.

CORKS AND SCREWS. Nothing is taken more for granted than the cork in the bottle. It is a natural product stripped from the bark of a cork oak, and it has been known for centuries, but no one thought of pressing it into the neck of a bottle until late in the sixteenth century. Yet its use has brought about a revolution in wine, for without it there would be no champagne, no ports, clarets, burgundies, or other great vintage wines. The earliest references to cork as a stopper suggest that the invention may have been English, and it came into use during the reign of Elizabeth I, but not into general use until later.

The oak that provides cork is the *querus suber* – an evergreen with comparatively small leaves, quite unlike the English oak. It grows in Mediterranean latitudes. The cork is obtained from the bark and it owes its remarkable properties to the fact that half if it is air: there are about two hundred million minute air-filled cells in a single cubic inch. It is these innumerable cavities that give corks their special characteristics of resilience and lightness, as well as being excellent heat insulators. So far as the use in a bottle is concerned, it is the closeness of the grain which distinguishes a quality cork, and the finest close grained cork is grown in the north-east of Spain, where the trees grow comparatively slowly so that the annual rings of growth are small.

It was not until the eighteenth century that cork came into its own, for two things had to occur: firstly the corkscrew (or 'bottlescrew' as it was at first known) had to be invented, and secondly the bottles had to evolve from broad based, misshapen decanters to the cylindrical bottles that we know today, capable of being binned on their sides; for wine has to be binned on its side if the cork is to remain moist and so keep airtight. The bottlescrew was invented at the beginning of the eighteenth century, no one knows by whom, and the bottle as we know it had come into existence by about 1770. Top quality vintage wines accordingly date from this period.

Some of the earlier corkscrews were very attractive looking things, with ivory handles at one end of which was a brush to brush away any dirt from the top of the bottle; and the screw itself consisted of a tapering metallic worm, the top of which ended in a platform to prevent the screw being driven too far into the cork. This style of corkscrew is still one of the best, and, generally speaking, a circular helix of metal (or worm) works better than the alternative formation of screw with a sharp cutting edge, as this only too often draws straight through the middle of an old and crumbly cork. One of the most practical forms consists of a box-wood frame with a left-handed screw serving to raise the cork after the corkscrew has been inserted. This makes a hard cork easier to remove, and it also helps to extract it gently. Other forms are made of metal, often with twin levers instead of the screw arrangement, and these work equally well. Perhaps the quickest is the zig-zag, or lazy-tongs corkscrew. Those who have the knack – and it needs a knack! – say that the two pronged extractor, which passes a piece of springy metal down either side of the cork, so that it can then gently be lifted out with a rotary movement, is the best of all for old corks. Finally there are the carbon dioxide or pneumatic devices. The carbon dioxide arrangement is excellent at wine parties where a great many corks have to be removed one after the other, but it is of doubtful efficiency on old corks, which sometimes break up rather dramatically under its influence. Pneumatic extractors, consisting of a small hand pump which pumps air down a tube inserted through the cork, are almost as quick, cost nothing to run, and are more reliable. There are, of course, many other fancy arrangements for corkscrews, some of them with almost unbelievable complications, but the standard article, with a good open worm, is perhaps as good as any.

CORTON   See BURGUNDY.

CORVO   See ITALIAN WINES.

COTEAUX DU LAYON   See LOIRE.

CÔTE DE BEAUNE   See BURGUNDY.

CÔTE DE NUITS   See BURGUNDY.

CÔTE D'OR   See BURGUNDY.

CÔTE ROTIE   See RHÔNE.

COULURE   A form of trouble with vines that is brought on by rain or cold weather. The blossoms are not pollinated so that the grapes do not develop, and fall off.

COUNTRY WINES   The rather vague name given to wines that are prepared in the country from all manner of things, some of the best known being cowslip, dandelion, elderberry, parsnip, rhubarb, and various fruits. Almost anything containing sugar can be fermented with the aid of yeast. Various kinds of flavouring are also added, and many of the older recipes actually advocate the addition of pure alcohol. 'French country wines' are grape wines from the lesser known areas. See FRANCE, THE LESSER KNOWN WINES.

CRADLES   The cradle is perhaps the most infuriatingly misapplied aid to wine drinking ever to have been invented. It has two uses: to help with decanting, or alternatively to avoid the need for decanting. Generally speaking, if there is time, decanting is best done by bringing the wine up from the cellar two or three days before it is required and then leaving the bottles to stand upright in a still place at the right temperature so that the sediment sinks to the bottom. The wine can then be decanted in the usual way (see DECANTERS AND DECANTING). But sometimes a red wine is needed in a greater hurry and then the host may bring the wine up out of the cellar in a basket, holding it very steadily, so that the wine is not shaken and the deposit remains in the position which it occupied in the cellar. The wine can then be decanted at any time by tilting the basket very gently and stopping before the sediment comes over. To avoid the need for decanting altogether, a bottle may be put into a basket (and this is particularly useful when the wine is very old and may fade rapidly in the glass or even during decanting) and then poured into the requisite number of glasses, holding the basket very steady so that the sediment does not get shaken up. But it is *essential* to complete the decanting in one operation. Once the cradle is put down, the wine swings back on to the sediment and stirs the whole thing up. There is nothing more infuriating than the misuse of decanting cradles in restaurants. To put a wine with no sediment in a cradle is an absurd affectation that takes up table space and serves no possible useful purpose. On the other hand, if the wine does have a sediment, it should be properly decanted as the perpetual movement of the basket, as glasses are refilled, inevitably stirs the sediment up. Any wine waiter bringing a bottle of red wine to a dining table in a cradle should have it slung at his head.

CRAVANT   See FRANCE, THE LESSER KNOWN WINES

CRÉMANT   A French term meaning slightly sparkling.

CRÈME DE MENTHE   See LIQUEUR.

CRÉPY   See FRANCE, THE LESSER KNOWN WINES.

CROIZES-HERMITAGE   See RHÔNE.

CRU   A French word meaning 'growth'.

CRUST   See DECANTING, PORT.

CUPS   There is nothing more refreshing or delightful for a summer party than a cool cup, nicely decorated with sprigs of mint or borage, with fruit in, and a little cucumber, to give a *look* of coolness. Best of all, it should have a trace of sparkle in it. Made in a vast jug or an open bowl, and served with a silver ladle, there can be nothing better to drink sitting on the lawn on a sunny day.

The most famous cups of all, of course, are Pimms, which are easy to prepare (just follow the directions on the bottle), delicious to drink, and highly deceptive – for they taste light and refreshing, but are very alcoholic nevertheless. Pimms No. 1, which is gin based, (a gin sling) is by far the most popular, but there are six to choose from. No. 2 is whisky, No. 3 is brandy, No. 4 is rum, No. 5 is rye, and No. 6 is vodka.

In mixing other cups, there is one golden rule to remember: do not be mean. Nothing tastes more futile than one that is over diluted. Here are some popular recipes.

Balaclava. Squeeze the juice of two lemons into a bowl and add the rind of half a lemon, free of pith. Sweeten with two tablespoonfuls of icing sugar and add a good handful of thin cucumber slices with the peel left on. Then add two bottles of cheap claret and mix well. Just before serving add ice, the contents of a siphon of soda water, and a bottle of a dry sparkling wine.

Champagne cup. For each bottle of champagne add a glass of brandy, two orange slices and a little lemon peel. Decorate with cucumber and borage (if you have any), or mint. Ice well. The flavour may be adjusted to taste by adding, optionally, liqueur glasses of Curaçao, Maraschino, or Grand Marnier.

Cider Cup. This recipe is by no means the most economical, but is one of the best. Put plenty of fruit in the bottom of a bowl. Oranges, lemons and peaches are perhaps the best, but a tin of pineapple also gives good results. Add half a bottle of brandy and half a bottle of cheap dry sherry, or of a sherry style wine from the Commonwealth. Leave for half an hour so that the liquid absorbs the flavour of the fruit. Then add plenty of ice and two flagons of sparkling cider.

Claret Cup. To each bottle of claret add a glass of Curaçao, and sweeten to taste with icing sugar. Then double the quantity by adding soda water. Ice and decorate in the usual way. For a better, stronger and more exotic claret cup, dry sparkling wine may be used instead of soda water.

Frugivorous wine cup. Put a mixture of sliced fresh fruits and a sprig of mint into a bowl and add one bottle of Alsatian riesling, a bottle of cheap red wine, and a miniature of apricot brandy. Sweeten to taste with icing sugar. Just before serving, add ice and a syphon of soda water.

Hock cup. To one bottle of hock add three glasses of sherry and a sliced lemon. Sweeten to taste with icing sugar. Then leave it for half an hour for the ingredients to mix before adding an equal quantity of soda water, ice and the usual decorations.

Vermouth quencher. Put a sliced lemon and ice in the bottom of a bowl. Add a bottle of dry vermouth and Crème de Cassis to taste – probably about two sherry glasses will be found about right, or if you do not have any Crème de Cassis, a mixture of two parts blackcurrant juice to one part brandy will do almost as well. Add a little icing sugar, if desired. Just before serving add four splits of fizzy lemonade. See also SANGRIA.

CURAÇAO   See LIQUEURS.

CUVÉE   The contents of a vat; a blend.

CYPRUS WINES   Anything written about the wines of Cyprus at the present moment is likely to seem hopelessly out of date in ten years' time, for recently there have been efforts to resuscitate the wine industry there and to regain the ancient renown that Cypriot wines once enjoyed. In particular this island enjoys an advantage practically unique in Europe in that the phylloxera has not yet made its way there. Newly imported varieties of vine, such as the Spanish Palomino, are now being grown, and there can be little doubt that new first class wines will be produced there, but so far few examples have been exported.

The finest of the traditional wines is commaderia – a brown, sweet dessert wine – and very good it is. It is a pity that sweet wines of this kind are so under-rated in Britain. Red table wines include those known as Olympus and as Othello. They are strong and heady. A sweetish fortified wine is sold unfortunately as 'Cyprus Sherry' – for its resemblance to the Spanish wine is very slight.

CZECHOSLOVAKIA Production is small and very little is exported. The white wines are the best, particularly those grown in Moravia.

DAIQUIRI See COCKTAIL.

DÂO See PORTUGUESE TABLE WINES.

DECANTERS AND DECANTING There is nothing more decorative on a table than a fine glass decanter resting on its silver coaster (which see). Decanters come in all shapes and sizes and have been made in all periods: the fat-bellied cut glass Georgian decanter, the conical shaped, flat-bottomed 'ship's decanter', that no one can knock over; or the exquisitely plain modern crystal decanters. All of these, in their different ways, represent glassware at its best, and the perfectly laid table seems somehow inadequate without them.

But are decanters really necessary? So far as spirits, sherry, wood port, and white table wines are concerned, a decanter serves no useful purpose whatsoever. In fact decanters are far less airtight then a well corked bottle, and sherry deteriorates in a decanter more quickly. But this does not matter if the wine is to be drunk at once, and anyhow decanters look so decorative. As far as red wines are concerned, however, decanters serve a very useful purpose. Such wines invariably throw a deposit with age, and if this is allowed to remain in the wine, it is spoilt – at any rate visually. Admittedly, if the deposit has settled well and the bottle is not shaken while the wine is being served, this will only affect the last glass or so that is poured out, but it is obviously more convenient to be able to pour out the whole of the wine at dinner without having to think carefully towards the end, and for this purpose it is sensible to decant it. So far as red table wine is concerned, this is best done by holding the bottle above a candle or low powered electric light and tilting it very gently, so that the wine pours into the decanter, while looking through the wine with the aid of this light, placed just short of the neck of the bottle. Towards the end, a streak of sediment will be seen approaching. It is here that the decanting should be stopped just before the sediment can get out. Vintage and crusted port call for a rather different treatment. The very large sediment that this kind of wine throws tends to cling to the side of the bottle, forming a crust, and occasionally quite large pieces become detached as the bottle is being poured out, whereas occasionally absolutely no sediment emerges, as the crust remains completely intact. In decanting port, therefore, it is advisable to use a silver funnel with small perforations in the bottom; such funnels are still made today and older ones are found in many most attractive designs in antique shops. Alternatively, a piece of clean muslin or linen can be used draped over a glass funnel. The perforations are small enough to prevent any detached pieces of crust from going through, and very often the whole of the wine can be passed into the decanter, though the bottle should immediately be tilted back if, towards the end, small pieces of sediment are seen to flow over.

But quite apart from the need to remove sediment, red wine is usually improved by decanting – and this goes for very young red wines which have not yet thrown any deposit – as the wine is aerated and the bouquet enhanced. The time that it is best to decant a wine depends very much on the vintage. Very old and mature clearets, for example, should be decanted immediately before they are served, as they can fade very rapidly, whereas a tough hard vintage, even if quite old, such as a 1937 or a 1945, could with advantage be decanted an hour or two before the time of dinner. Very young wines may be decanted half a day beforehand. The stopper can then be left out of the decanter so that the wine can 'breathe'. There is a rival school of thought, it must be admitted, that regards decanting purely as an affectation when applied to young wines that have little or no deposit. I can only say that I do not subscribe to it.

DEIDESHEIM   See RHINE.

DEMI-SEC   Half dry, literally, but in practice sweet.

DESSERT WINE   A sweet wine suitable for drinking with the dessert.

DISTILLATION AND RECTIFICATION   Alcohol mixes with water in any proportion, but fortunately alcohol distils at a lower temperature than water, and when the mixture is boiled the alcohol comes off first in the form of a vapour. This is the basis of distillation. A fermented alcoholic liquid is placed in a receptacle called the still which is slowly heated, and the vapour rising is then condensed. The old-fashioned form of still, known as the pot-still (which is essentially the same as the alchemist's alembic), needs to be cooled and refilled after each distillation, and quite a lot of 'impurities', or congenerics, are driven off and condensed with the alcohol. It is these, arising from the liquid which is being djstilled, that give the various spirits their characteristic flavours. Alternatively a patent or Coffey still (name after Aeneas Coffey, a customs official who invented it) may be used, which provides a continuous process that is much cheaper. The alcohol condensing from a patent still is much purer than that from a pot still and hence is lighter in flavour and quicker to mature. Pot stills are used for distilling cognac, armagnac, malt whisky, and Irish whisky, whereas grain whisky is distilled by the patent process. Commercial branded whiskies are blends of malt and grain in varying proportions (see WHISKY).

Rectification is the process of distilling a liquid which has already been distilled. The object may be to secure an alcohol which is as pure as possible, and is known as rectified spirit. Such tasteless alcohols are used, for example, in compounding vodka. Alternatively the rectification may be conducted with various flavouring agents combined with the alcohol in the still so that their flavours enter the rectified spirit to produce, for example, gin or a liqueur (which see).

DOMAINE   Estate, especially in Burgundy.

DORDOGNE   See FRANCE, THE LESSER KNOWN WINES.

DOUX   Sweet.

DRAMBUIE   See LIQUEUR.

DUBONNET   See APERITIF.

EAST INDIA   In the days of sailing boats, casks of sherry and madeira were sometimes sent on voyages to the East Indies and back because it was found that the varying temperature and rocking of the boat helped to mature them and give them a special quality. The term is still sometimes used in connection with sherry to indicate a sweet, dark wine, but such wines are no longer matured in the traditional way.

EAUX-DE-VIE   Literally this means 'waters of life' and in fact simply signifies a spirit obtained from the distillation from any alcoholic fermentation, for such distillates were, in the old days of alchemy, thought to be the waters of life. For example eaux-de-vie de marc is a spirit distilled from the husk of grapes or MARC.

ECHÉZEAUX   See BURGUNDY.

EISWEIN   See GERMAN WINE TERMS.

ELTVILLE   See RHINE.

ENOLOGY (OR OENOLOGY)   A study of wine making.

ENOTECA AT SIENA   See ITALIAN WINES.

ENTRE-DEUX-MERS   See BORDEAUX, WHITE.

ERDEN   See MOSELLE.

EST! EST!! EST!!!   See ITALIAN WINES.

FALERNO   See ITALIAN WINES.

FINGER LAKES   See AMERICAN WINES.

FINING   The process of clarifying a liquid by precipitating floating particles. Various agents are used such as white of egg and isinglass, though nowadays it is more usual to use one of the many patent finings or to rely on efficient modern filtration.

FINO   See SHERRY.

FIRING GLASS   A glass with a thick bottom used by freemasons to bang on the table in acknowledgement of a toast.

FIXIN   See BURGUNDY.

FIZZES   Fizzes are long cocktails given effervescence, for the most part, by soda water. There is one notable exception to this, Buck's Fizz, which is probably the best of the lot. To make it, pour the juice of a freshly squeezed orange into a wine glass and fill up with champagne. In practise it tastes just as good, and costs considerably less, if the champagne is replaced by a lesser, dry sparkling wine. The basic kind of fizz – and one of the best – is a gin fizz. To make this put the juice of half a lemon and one wine glass of gin in a cocktail shaker with crushed ice and a teaspoonful of icing sugar. After shaking, pour into a tumbler and fill up with cold soda water. Serve immediately. A cream fizz is the same thing with a teaspoonful of fresh cream added to the shaker. To make a golden fizz, use the yolk of an egg instead of cream. Any book of cocktail recipes will give many more versions, most of which are varied by adding such things as dashes of maraschino, orange-juice, lime-juice, grenadine syrup, and so forth. Brandy, rum, or whisky, may be used in place of gin.

FLEURIE   See BURGUNDY.

FLOR   See SHERRY.

FOOD, WINE WITH   There is only one rule about choosing wine to go with food: to remember that no matter what anyone may say, there is no such thing as a rule. Far too much pedantic nonsensense has been written on the subject in the past, and no doubt a great deal more will be in the future. If you happen to favour some bizarre combination like claret and kippers, you have every right to do so, and anyone who attempts to deny you the right is a fool; but as a courtesy to one's guests it is generally desirable to be more conventional when giving a dinner party, and it is also usually a good idea to try the accepted partnerships first. They are accepted simply because people like them. The better eccentricities (and claret with kippers is not one of them) stem from knowledge and experience, rather than from ignorance. Choosing the right wine to go with food is an art – and the very thought is enough to put many people off. But it is not at all a difficult art to master, and there is a great deal of fun to be had in learning it. Such is the range of foods and wines in daily consumption that any list would be impossibly long and certainly inadequate. It is better to work on a basis of common sense and experience. All one needs is to have a reasonable memory for flavours and to bear in mind that, unless one is trying to be bold, flavours should harmonise rather than clash. It is not necessary to deal with the finer subtleties: anyone who has reached that stage will want no advice anyhow. In this entry I shall simply give some idea of my own tastes.

There are some things, of course, that positively no wine will go with: herrings, for instance, and very hot curries. Water, cider or beer (especially lager with curries) are generally the best bets. It would be absurd to drink a really fine wine with any sort of curry as its finer qualities would never be perceived and it would be wasted. It is astounding, though, how well a dry white wine will stand up to a curry, a muscadet, for instance, or an alsatian. The alternative would be a cheap robust red wine, like a Chilean. Egg dishes are not easy to match with wines, either, as they tend to be too sulphury; and vinegar is the enemy of wine – especially malt vinegar. Most dishes go with some sort of wine, though, if you are prepared to think for a minute; and some wines are remarkably easy about the dishes that they go with. The easiest of the lot is champagne, which goes with almost everything. And some wines exist with such a wide range of flavours that their devotees say that an example can be found to go with any dish. This claim is frequently made on behalf of hock, and while I am prepared to agree that there is quite a lot of justification in it, nevertheless I am far happier to have a glass of good red wine with a red, juicy steak.

The old rule used to be 'red wine with red meat and white wine with white meat'. That is all right so far as it goes, and there are few who would dispute its first limb, but the second raises many doubts. In the first place, what is 'white meat'? Would a lawyer construe this as including fish, poultry, and game? If so, it is full of pitfalls.

Perhaps it would be wiser to begin at the beginning of the meal. With soup it is generally best to have dry sherry or

madeira, and sherry is one of the few wines which will stand up
to a highly spiced hors d'oeuvres. A less assertive hors d'oeuvres,
especially one with the emphasis on fish, goes very well with a
dry, light white wine but the possibilities, with hors d'oeuvres,
themselves being so variable in composition, are so wide that
they could almost run the whole gamut of available wines. For
oysters, the classic wines are champagne and chablis, though
other dry white wines taste very well and some prefer stout. For
my own taste, fish in any form calls for a dry, or a fairly dry,
white wine, though there are some who favour red wines with
salmon or red mullet and this has been pointed out so often that
the combination is now an accepted eccentricity. With salmon
a lot depends on how it is cooked. A grilled salmon steak is
so meaty that claret tastes well with it. The best example of a
white meat I can think of is veal, and I think that the old saying
is justified, for despite the fact that many people enjoy claret with
their veal, for my own part I prefer a white wine, preferably a
hock or white burgundy. Pork is more difficult, for no wine
shows really to advantage against it. A fairly cheap dryish white
wine is probably the best bet, or the opposite extreme,
an old, fine burgundy. Is lamb a white meat or red one? Which
ever it be, my own preference is undoubtedly for red wine,
and the perfect match is surely claret? Beef is undoubtedly
red, and there I should choose claret or burgundy depending on
the cut; claret with a fillet steak, for example, and burgundy
with the stronger flavour of a rump. If the words 'white meat'
are held to include poultry, then I disagree with the old saying,
for to my own taste a roast chicken goes perfectly with claret,
though I will happily accept that it goes very well with the dry
white wines, such as white burgundy, while boiled chicken certainly calls for a white wine. With roast turkey I have found a
light red burgundy very pleasant. Game is a subject on its own,
for the flavours provided can vary so enormously. For my own
taste the wine should be red, but it is more difficult than that.
With a lightly hung pheasant or partridge, a claret is ideal, but
with a very flavoury game pie one needs a burgundy, while with
some versions of jugged hare, something even more robust from
the Rhône is called for. Highly flavoured dishes always call for
the most thought, and some are very difficult to match indeed,
such as goulash. With this, perhaps as good a bet as any is the

Hungarian red wine called bull's blood. It also seems appropriate. Similarly, Italian wines seem to have the right cutting edge to penetrate the strong flavours of Italian dishes.

It has been suggested, wrongly I think, that 'any wine goes with any cheese' though, as with most of these sayings, there is certainly an element of truth in it. Some cheeses, such as Roquefort, seem to flatter many wines. Generally speaking wines that are light in flavour, such as white wines and claret, go best with cheeses that are relatively mild such as the white English cheeses, whereas a cheese so individualistic and powerful as Stilton tastes best when accompanied by an equally vigorous wine, such as port. Port also goes extremely well with nuts and with apples.

It is a pity that more people do not try and produce a wine to go with the pudding course. Some puddings of course, such as those that are swimming in honey, would overpower absolutely any wine, and it is hopeless to try. But most pastries, and concoctions that are not covered with syrups and jams, make excellent accompaniements for those very under-rated sweet white wines such as a good sauternes or barsac.

This entry has gone on quite long enough, but it has only just touched on the fringe of the subject. There are only four things to remember, though: use your memory, experiment a little, don't be nervous about it, and ignore the pedantries of wine snobs.

FORST See THE RHINE.

FORTIFICATION This consits of increasing the strength of wine by adding alcohol at the time of vinification, either before or after the fermentation is complete, depending on the style of wine which is to be produced. If a sweet wine is required, the alcohol, or a certain proportion of it, is generally added before the fermentation is complete, as this arrests the fermentation process before all the natural sugar of the must has been used up and converted into alcohol. Conversely, if a completely dry wine is required, the alcohol must be added afterwards. The best known of the fortified wines are sherry, port, madeira, and marsala.

FOXY This has nothing to do with foxes. The native American grape was designated the 'fox grape'. Wines made from it have a very characteristic aroma and flavour as do wines made from grapes grown on many of the vines descended from it by breeding or hybridization. This is described as foxiness and such wines are said to be foxy.

FRAMBOISE See LIQUEURS.

FRANCE

1 Calvados. 2 Champagne. 3 Alsace. 4 Muscadet. 5 Anjou. 6 Sancerre. 7 Reuilly. 8 Quincy. 9 Pouilly-sur-Loire. 10 Chablis. 11 Côtes de Nuits, Côtes de Beaune. 12 Nuits St George. 13 Beaune. 14 Côtes de Jura. 15 Beaujolais. 16 Côtes du Rhône. 17 Clairette de Die. 18 Cassis, Bandol. 19 Cognac. 20 Bergerac. 21 Bordeaux. 22 Armagnac. 23 Jurançon. 24 Gaillac. 25 Blanquette de Limoux. 26 Roussillon.

FRANCE, THE LESSER KNOWN WINES As every traveller knows, the lesser known wines of France are legion – and it all depends on what you mean by 'lesser known'. The wines of Alsace, the Loire and the Rhône are themselves lesser known than those of, for example, Bordeaux and Burgundy, but they are nevertheless so well known that they receive entries to themselves. The only part of France where no noteworthy wine is grown is the north-west where cider is grown instead. The south-west region is on the whole temperate, influenced by the Atlantic, and the most famous wine growing area in that region is of course Bordeaux. Moving inland from Bordeaux, the wines of the Dordogne and of the Lot are not dissimilar in style, are grown in large quantities, and are well worth looking for. The principal area for red wines is around Bergerac, while the most famous white wine of the Dordogne is monbazillac; it is comparable with sauternes but slightly less sweet, less full-flavoured, and less aromatic. It ages well and is a notable dessert wine. The Lot grows excellent wines and perhaps the best known is 'the black wine of Cahors'. To call it 'black' is perhaps an exaggeration, though it is certainly a very deep red. In the past such wines were probably blacker than they are today. The best are wines of very real distinction that need many years to mature properly. Moving further south, the enchanting countryside from Pau to the Pyrenees is perhaps more notable for its landscape than for its wines, but some of them, nevertheless, are worth looking for. The most famous is jurançon grown to the south and west of Pau. It has a very fruity flavour with a remarkable, fragrant and subtle bouquet that quite defies description, and it ages very well. In the past it was always rather sweet, but modern growers are tending to produce somewhat drier wines, though sweet wines are still made, especially in the sunniest years. The region of Gaillac lies well to the north-east, and its wines were once amongst the most widely exported from France, but that was a long time ago and they have hardly been known in this country since the end of the seventeenth century. In the past the red wines were particularly famous but today the region is almost entirely known for its white wines, which are grown in every degree of sweetness and which tend to be bottled in the shape of bottle normally associated with hock. Sparkling wines and fortified wines are also produced there.

The great wines of northern France are of course Champagne and the isolated oasis of Chablis, near the mediaeval town of Auxerre. The Chablis vineyards are so surpassingly famous that their neighbours are almost forgotten, at least abroad. Nevertheless they grow some pleasant wines. Some interesting red wines, for example, are grown around Auxerre, Cravant and Irancy, but the clay soil gives some of them a very powerful flavour – so much so that they are an acquired taste – while others seem thin and acid. Nowadays more and more of the wine is being vinified as *rosé* and is being exported.

Travelling east from Burgundy one crosses over a wide dull plain then the mountains begin to rise again as one approaches Switzerland, and here are the vineyards of the Jura. The most popular wines of this area are the rosés, grown around Arbois, and the greatest are the *vins jaunes*, otherwise known as *vins de garde*, which are undoubtedly amongst the great wines of Europe. They are quite unlike any other French wines, and the only other wine that comes near to them in character is sherry – way down on the south of Spain. The greatest *vin jaune* of all is Château-Chalon – which is not a Château in the Bordeaux sense: it is the name of a village and that of a whole, rather sparsely planted, district. Like sherry, these wines last almost for ever, but the comparison must not be carried too far: they have a very attractive flavour that is all their own, and it is their misfortune that they are so readily compared with the more popular wine. Although they are not fortified, they are very strong. Of the other wines, the white ones tend to be too flat, or too thin and acid for my taste, and this acidity is also apparent in some of the reds, but others have real character and are excellent to drink, though not rising to great heights.

To the south of the Jura lie the vineyards of the Savoy around the upper reaches of the Rhône and by Annecy. Both red and white wines are grown, but although the former are pleasant enough, it is the latter that are worth looking for, especially aprémont, seyssel and, to a lesser extent, crépy, and roussette. These wines bridge the gap in character as well as in geography between those of France and those of Switzerland. They want drinking young, and some are slightly *pétillant*, while others, unfortunately, are deliberately made *mousseux*.

Turning to the south of France, the wines tend to remind one of the old truism that it is the struggle for survival that produces character. Most of them have no struggle and little character. In Provence the best red wine is that of Bandol which may be compared with châteauneuf-du-pape. The best known white wines come from Cassis, nearby; these are generally dry, full of flavour,

and strong. They must on no account be confused with the
alcoholic blackcurrant syrup of Dijon, which has the same name
and which is popular as an aperitif when mixed with white wine.
Bellet, above Nice, grows principally a white wine that is renowned locally, while Palette, inland near Aix, provides quite
good red, white and rosé wines. On the whole, however, it is
the rosé wines of Provence that are the most popular. They taste
delicious on the spot, well-chilled and drunk beneath the sun;
and they are now being exported on quite a substantial scale.
Most of them are very dry, and they tend to be strong in flavour.

The areas of Languedoc and Roussillon are noted for quantity
rather than quality, though there is an occasional exception which
rises to mediocrity. Quite a good red wine is grown near
Montpelier, while Lunel and Frontignan produce two of the best
muscats of France. A sparkling white wine known as blanquette
de limoux is grown somewhat inland near Limoux, and although
it is notoriously variably in quality, it can be quite pleasant.

These are but a few of the lesser known wines of France;
there are many, many more. Some travel and some do not, but
nearly all of them can be enjoyed in their own country. They
taste best there, and the local cooks know how to complement
them with their dishes. There is no more pleasant way to spend a
holiday than to wander gently around France, drinking diligently
all the way. But the traveller should beware. A wine that tastes
admirable on the spot, drunk beneath the sun on a terrace over-
looking the Mediterranean, often tastes perfectly filthy when
drunk surrounded by a London fog. Most of the lesser known
wines that are really worth importing are already being imported,
and while obliging wine merchants may go to a lot of trouble to
import some local wine that has caught a traveller's fancy, nine
times out of ten the traveller will find that he has made an
expensive mistake in persuading his wine merchant to do so.

FRANCONIA Franconian wines are undoubtedly some of Germany's best, though few would dare to suggest that they compare
with the great growths of the Rhine and Moselle. Their rather
steely flavour is inclined to be somewhat flat and to lack that
exquisite complexity that distinguishes Germany's greatest wines;
but even so, in the best years (which are not always the same as
those for Rhine wines) Franconian wines can be very good indeed.

Part of their popularity no doubt stems from the beautiful flask-shaped *bocksbeutels* in which they are bottled. They are grown in the valley of the Main and the finest wines are derived, as might be expected, from Riesling grapes. They are often known as *Steinweins*, but this term is used far too loosely, and should only be applied to wines grown in the large and very fine Stein site at Würzburg. The nearby Leisten vineyard produces equally good wines, and there are several others that do not lag far behind.

FRASCATI   See ITALIAN WINES.

FRONSAC   See CLARET.

FRONTIGNAN   See FRANCE, THE LESSER KNOWN WINES.

GAILLAC   See FRANCE, THE LESSER KNOWN WINES.

GATTINARA   See ITALIAN WINES.

GEISENHEIM   See RHINE.

GENEVA   Gin (which has no connection with the Swiss city); a corruption of jenever (juniper).

GERMAN WINE TERMS   The four fundamental terms used in describing German wines are: *spätlese, auslese, beerenauslese,* and *trockenbeerenauslese.* A spätlese wine is a wine made towards the end of the vintage, and which has had no sugar added to increase its strength or sweetness artificially. An auslese wine is made with select bunches of over ripe grapes. If over ripe berries are selected instead of bunches of grapes, it is called a beeren-auslese. And finally if individual berries are picked which are so shrivelled as to be practically like raisins, the wine is a *trocken-beerenauslese.* Each of these stages represents a further step of richness, and a trockenbeerenauslese is so luscious that it is more like a liqueur than a table wine. Other terms used in describing German wines include:
abfüllung: bottling.
abzug: bottling.
auslese: selected bunches of grapes (see above).
beerenauslese: selected berries (see above).

cabinet, cabinetwein: the best wine produced by the grower concerned.

creszens: vineyard the property of the person named. This term may only be applied to unsugared wine.

echt: genuine. This term may only be applied to unsugared wine.

edelauslese: a noble auslese.

edelbeerenauslese: see beerenauslese.

edelgewächs: a noble wine.

eiswein: literally, ice wine; wines made from grapes which have been frozen naturally by the frost, and which are then pressed before they thaw. This results in a peculiarly rich must, giving a rather sweet wine having a characteristic flavour that is much sought after.

erben: heirs.

erzenger abfüllung: bottled by the producers.

fass nr: cask number. This term may only be applied to unsugared wine.

feine: finest.

fuder nr: cask number. This term may only be applied to unsugared wines from the Moselle.

gebiet: region.

gewächs: growth. This term may only be applied to unsugared wine.

goldbeerenauslese: this is not a beerenauslese but an auslese made from fully ripe, golden grapes.

hock: a rhine wine – term used only in English.

kabinett, kabinettwein: the best wine produced by the grower concerned.

kellerabfüllung or *kellerabzug:* bottled in the cellar named.

kellerei: cellars.

kreszenz: vineyard the property of the person named. This term may only be applied to unsugared wine.

Liebfraumilch or *Liebfrauenmilch:* a term much beloved of the English, but one that is generally to be deplored. It is generally thought to mean 'Our Lady's Milk' and was originally closely associated with the vineyards around the Liebfrauenkirche at Worms, but it is now applied loosely to blended German wines, generally from the Rheinhessan. Such wines are commercially popular and invariably pleasant but they are never great, nor do they provide such good value as others that the discriminating are able to select.

Moselblumchen: the Moselle equivalent of Liebfraumilch.

naturrein: as naturwein.

naturwein: a natural wine made without sugaring, and un-blended. This is assumed where the wine is spätlese or above, but the fact that it is a naturwein may be added for emphasis.

original original. Thus originwein – original wine; original – abfüllung or originalabzug – original bottling; and so on. A wine may only be described as an original bottling if it is unsugared and is matured and bottled in the grower's cellars.

perlwein: a wine made to be slightly bubbly.

qualitaetswein: quality wine made in a declared region.

qualitaeswein mit praedikα.: quality wine of special distinction.

rotwein: red wine.

schaumwein: a second quality sparkling wine. If containing added carbon dioxide, the words 'mit zugesetzer kohlensaeure' are added.

schlossabfüllung or *schlossabzug:* bottled at the castle.

sekt: sparkling wine.

spätlese: late gathered (see above).

trockenbeerenauslese: selected very ripe berries (see above).

verbesserte: literally 'bettered'; in fact, chaptalized – that is to say sugar is added to the must to make up a deficiency in the grapes in poor years.

wachstum: vineyard the property of the person named. This term may only be applied to unsugared wine.

wein: wine.

weingut: estate. But this does not mean that the wine is estate bottled.

winzergenossenschaft: co-operative.

winzerverein: co-operative.

Once these terms have been understood the complex German wine label immediately ceases from being incomprehensible; in fact one is struck by its lucidity and pedantic accuracy as com-pared with the labels from the other great areas. The information is put down in the following order: first the town or village, which generally has the suffix -er added to its name; then the particular vineyard site (the *lagen*); then the grape; then details as to the time of picking, for instance whether the wine was an auslese; then any appropriate details as to the grower, etc.; and then, of course, the vintage. Thus Oestricher Lenchen Riesling Spätlese Cabinet 1959 is a late gathered cabinet wine of the 1959 vintage, grown in the Lenchen vineyard at Oestrich. And so on. All the really fine German wines, coming from leading vineyards, will have the vineyard name specified on the label. The absence of such a name always means that the wine is not in the top class, and usually that it is a blend. But beware of certain vineyard names. Recently the rules have been relaxed, and although the vineyard name still means just what it says on estate bottled wines, on others certain vineyard names no longer have any more than a generic meaning.

As far as the town or village is concerned, moreover, the use of its name without a specific site name does not mean that the wine has come from the vineyards adjoining the town; the major centres of wine growing are allowed to apply their names to any wine of the appropriate style, quality, and value (of which the shipper is the sole judge) grown 'adjacent or near' to them, which in practice means within ten miles. Thus a wine labelled 'bernkasteler' may have been grown up to ten miles from Bernkastle.

GERMANY, THE LESSER KNOWN WINES. Germany, is, of course, the most northerly of the major wine growing countries of Europe. In consequence, the hazards besetting the wine grower are far greater than in most other countries, and the quality of the vintage is extremely unpredictable. This causes the wines to be expensive, but the wine grower is compensated by the fact that they are peculiarly fine and delicate, so that they can command extremely high prices. Were it not for this, wine growing in Germany would hardly be an economic proposition. In buying a German wine one is faced from the outset with the fact that one must pay a relatively high price for it, and consequently the wine must be good if the price is to be justified. Generally speaking, the major districts, which have individual entries, provide what are by far the greatest wines, and the quality of these is such that it is scarcely worth while importing wines from other regions, though a certain amount is now being imported from Baden, and very good it is too. Few of the other wines will be found outside

GERMANY

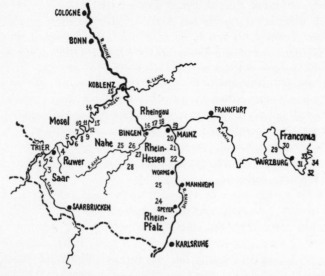

1 Saarburg, Ayl, Wawern, Kanzem. 2 Wiltingen. 3 Serrig, Ockfen. 4 Kasel, Mertesdorf, Eitelsbach. 5 Piesport, Trittenheim. 6 Dhron, Neumagen. 7 Wehlen, Lieser. 8 Bernkastel, Brauneberg, Wintrich. 9 Erden, Zeltingen, Graach, Trarbach. 10 Uerzig. 11 Traben. 12 Enkirch. 13 Zell. 14 Kochem, Eller. 15 Winningen. 16 Assmannshausen, Rüdesheim. 17 Hallgarten, Johannisberg, Geisenheim, Winkel, Oestrich, Hattenheim. 18 Kiedrich, Rauenthal, Erbach, Eltville. 19 Hochheim. 20 Laubenheim, Bodenheim, Nackenheim. 21 Nierstein, Oppenheim. 22 Guntersblum, Alsheim, Mettenheim. 23 Kallstadt, Bad Dürkheim. 24 Wachenheim, Forst, Deidesheim, Ruppertsberg, Königsbach, Neustadt. 25 Böckelheim, Norheim. 26 Roxheim, Winzerheim, Münster am Stein. 27 Kreuznach. 28 Niederhausen. 29 Himmelstadt. 30 Retzbach. 31 Randersacker, Dettelbach. 32 Rödelsee, Iphofen. 33 Escherndorf. 34 Sommerach.

Germany, but if one is in that country, they are well worth looking for, and wine growing is far more widespread than one might think. The climatic conditions which give the white wines their unique delicacy, however, make the country quite unsuitable for growing really high quality red wines. Some of the German red wines enjoy local esteem and are praised beyond the bounds of reason by local advocates, but on the whole these are to be avoided. A certain amount of red wine is grown on the Rheingau at Assmannshausen, but to my own taste it gives the impression of aspiring unsuccessfully to be white; its redness is a disguise, worn

72

thinly; it tastes rather like a second rate hock with a dash of burgundy. Another district noted for its red wine is Ahr, but although different from the red wines of Assmannshausen, these strike me as being no better. Some of the most attractive of the lesser German wines are those grown around Lake Constance, especially weissherbst – a wine of the palest pink, such as the French would call a *vin gris*, vinified from the Pinot Noir. Baden and Württemberg grow both red and white wines, of which some of the white are really good. The red wines are rather slight and more like full bodied rosés than real reds. Those Baden wines that are grown between Wiesloch and Weinheim are known as *bergstrasse*, the best of which comes from the Steinhopf vineyard in Heppenheim. See also FRANCONIA.

GEROPIGA A very sweet wine made in Portugal by inhibiting fermentation of must. It is used in blending and sometimes sold for drinking.

GEVREY-CHAMBERTIN See BURGUNDY.

GIGONDAS See RHÔNE.

GIN One of the most popular of all drinks, this is one of the latest to have arrived on the scene, since it was unknown in England until the middle of the seventeenth century. It was probably originally distilled in Holland, and was for a long time known as 'Hollands'. It became of considerable commercial significance at the end of the seventeenth and at the beginning of the eighteenth century thanks largely to government interference which imposed prohibitive taxes on French wines. The result was disastrous. The early gins were undoubtedly of abominable quality and seriously deleterious to the health. Perhaps the most notorious advertisement of all time was that which read 'Drunk for a penny. Dead drunk for twopence. Fresh straw every day', but the most eloquent condemnation of all was that of Hogarth in his picture 'Gin Lane'. By the end of the eighteenth century, more enlightened legislation had largely put the matter to rights though the stigma that attached to gin remained well into the nineteenth century, and only left it in the cocktail era of he 1920s. It is now as popular as it is respectable. Its name is derived from the French *genièvre*, or the Dutch *jeneves* both meaning juniper, which was corrupted first into *Geneva* and then *gin*; but the English word has predominated and is now regularly used in French. Gin begins as a completely neutral spirit, and although a grain spirit is generally used in practice, other spirits are perfectly suitable. It is flavoured by being re-distilled, or rectified, with juniper berries and other secret ingredients, according to the recipe of the maker. Coriander is another of the flavouring agents which is known to be employed. Collectively they are known as 'botanicals'. London Dry Gin, made this way, has peculiarly clean and uncomplicated flavour. At the other end of the scale is Dutch Gin, which is still sometimes referred to as Hollands, and is often sold in stone jars or crocks. In making this kind of gin the original spirit is not rectified, so that it retains some of its grain flavour and needs to be matured before being sold. It is also generally distilled at lower strength, and the Dutch enjoy drinking it neat, often out of tall narrow glasses. Somewhere in between the two styles is Plymouth Gin, which is often particularly favoured for making pink gin, by adding a dash of angostura bitters. Certain flavoured gins are also sold for use as liqueurs, some based on London gin and others on Dutch. The most famous is probably sloe gin, but lemon gin and orange gin are also popular and ginger gin is sometimes found.

GINGER Ginger is an extremely popular flavouring agent owing to its warm flavour, which is particularly appropriate to the British climate. Some ginger drinks, such as ginger ale, are wholly unalcoholic, relying simply on essence of ginger to provide them with their flavour. Ginger beer, however, is alcoholic – though the commercial versions are only very slightly so, having an upper limit of 2 per cent alcohol. It is made by fermenting ginger with sugar and yeast, and although the commercial kind is necessarily very weak in alcohol in order to avoid duty, a strong ginger beer can quite easily be made in the home. Ginger wine is also popular in this country, and although it used to be made in the home, most of it is now made commercially, using imported must which is fermented and flavoured with ginger. It is also used for flavouring liqueurs such as 'King's Ginger Liqueur' and ginger gin.

GLASSES A great deal of nonsense has been written on the subject of wine glasses. In the last century, and in the early years of this century particularly, manufacturers of glasses and gift shops went out of their way to produce a different type of glass 'suitable' for every conceivable type of wine. Many of them were suitable for no wine at all, and to suggest that a different glass is necessary for each kind of wine is absurd. Basically, any good wine calls for a glass having certain definite characteristics: it should be absolutely clear and not embellished by too much decoration, so that the colour of the wine can be appreciated; it should be reasonably large so that an adequate amount can be put in, and an air space still left over the top for the bouquet to develop; it should be wider at the bottom than the top so that the wine can be swirled round safely and the bouquet kept in and concentrated, allowing this very important aspect of the flavour to be enjoyed; and it should preferably have a stem so that the glass is not fouled with finger marks, or the wine heated if it is intended to drink it cold. In other words, a tulip shaped glass is admirable for every sort of wine – a large tulip for table wines and a small one for fortified wines. The worst kind of wine glass imaginable is the heavily cut, saucer shaped glasses which used to be popular for champagne. They were completely disastrous. They gave the wine no chance to show its bouquet and let the bubbles escape far too quickly. A tulip shaped glass is admirable for champagne, but failing that some of the old flute shaped champagne glasses with a little diamond-cut at the bottom to give the bubbles a base on which to form themselves were excellent; and any tall glass which comes in a little towards the top, or which has parallel sides, will do very well. Being tall, it enables the bubbles to travel a substantial way up the wine and so to be more greatly appreciated. In Burgundy, the wines are often served in what appear to be exceptionally large balloon brandy glasses. These are really no more than an exaggeration of the tulip shape, but they are certainly admirable for drinking any table wine out of, as the large volume over the surface of wine, and the exaggerated curve inwards towards the top of the glass, enable the bouquet of the wine to be particularly well appreciated. The fashionable sherry *copita* is also simply a variation on the tulip theme, and is as excellent for port as it is for sherry. On no account insult either of these wines with the public house thimble in which they are so often served; no wine can possibly show to advantage in such a glass. The worst of the lot are those that go in at the middle and out again at the top. Other glasses are peculiarly pleasing to look at, and quite harmless to drink out of, such as the German *roemer* which is often recommended for Rhine wines. For brandy and liqueurs, it is hard to better the well known balloon shape, though the glass should be small so that a reasonable depth and not too great a surface of brandy are provided, and it should also be made out of extremely thin glass so that the fingers of the hand can warm the spirit and enhance its bouquet. See also FIRING GLASS.

GLENFIDDICH   A famous Highland malt whisky distilled at the Glenfiddich distillery on Speyside by the descendants of William Grant who, with his seven sons, built the distillery by hand in 1886. The only Highland malt bottled at the distillery.

GLENLIVET   A famous Scotch malt whisky, distilled by Smiths. The name is also applied to other excellent malt whiskies made by distillers in the same area, but these have the name hyphenated with that of the distiller or some suitable distinguishing mark.

GRAND MARNIER   See LIQUEUR.

GRAPPA   See MARC.

GREEK WINE   Greece is a wine-growing country of supreme antiquity, but its achievements in wine, as in the fine arts, lie in the past rather than in the present. Today it produces large quantities of wines, most of which are mediocre and most of which are drunk locally. Amongst them are undoubtedly some good ones, since there is an active co-operative movement and there are a number of large, first-class commercial growers. Nevertheless, much of the wine is still made by peasants, and viticulture, judged by the standards of the fine wine regions of Europe, is haphazard and primitive. To many wine drinkers, Greece is synonymous with *retsina*: the resin flavoured wine which, perhaps because it is so different from the other table wines of Europe, has received the most publicity. There are various theories as to how this wine came to be made: some date it back to the Peloponnesian war, when Athens was infested by cholera and resin was added to the wine as a disinfectant, while others say that wine was once stored in casks made of pine wood, and the flavour which it imparted became so popular that from then onwards it was introduced on purpose. Neither theory seems very probable. The ancient Greeks and Romans certainly used many flavouring agents to blend with their wines, and perhaps from these efforts we can trace our modern vermouths and liqueurs, but with the exception of retsina, artificially flavoured table wines virtually disappeared. Whatever the history, wines have been treated with pine resin since the most ancient of times. The best retsinas are grown in Attica especially around Athens. Most of these are white, but also a certain amount of rosé retsina is made, though no red. Retsina does not improve in bottle and should be drunk young. Other red, white and rosé wines are grown in Attica, but none is particularly distinguished.

The most important wine growing region is the Peloponnese – both as regards quantity and quality. Although the table wines are of little interest, the dessert wines are quite good, particularly the muscat of Patras. Mavrodaphne is very sweet but of a rather medicinal flavour. Like Hungarian tokay, it should generally be drunk at room temperature, two very rare exceptions to the general rule that white dessert wines should be chilled.

The island of Samos, the birth place of Pythagoras, grows some of the best Greek wines, which are even favoured with a law of controlled appellation, not generally found elsewhere in Greece. The most popular grape is the muscat, and practically all the wine is well made in the co-operative. It comes in all degrees of sweetness. The driest is bone dry but nevertheless has the muscat nose more often associated with sweeter wines, and a very distinctive flavour that makes it rather an acquired taste – though less so than retsina. The best of all are the sweet dessert wines.

The great days of Greek wine undoubtedly lie in the remote past, and quite possibly in the not so remote future. Very serious attempts are being made to improve the standard of viticulture and to create laws of appellation. As things are at present, there are some excellent wines to be found, but they need to be sought out carefully.

Apart from table wines, Greece produces a number of aperitifs, liqueurs, and brandies. Of the aperitifs, Ouzo is by far the best known. It is a grape spirit flavoured with aniseed and various herbs. It is generally drunk with water and ice, in approximately the proportion of two parts Ouzo to one part water, and when the water is added, it turns cloudy. Masticha is grape spirit, flavoured with gum mastic, made on the island of Chios, and although often listed as an aperitif is also drunk as a liqueur. Brandies are also produced in quite large quantities.

GRIS   Very pale rosé.

GROG   Rum and water; sometimes heated and spiced, with or without lemon. Called after Admiral Vernon, whose nickname was 'Old Grog'.

GRUMELLO   See ITALIAN WINES.

HALLGARTEN   See RHINE.

HERMITAGE   See RHÔNE.

HESSIA   See RHINE (Rheinhessen).

HIPPOCRAS   A concoction of wine and honey, popular in the Middle Ages.

HOCHHEIM   See RHINE.

HOCK   A word existing only in English and synonymous with Rhine wine, which see.

HOLLANDS   See GIN.

HOSPICES DE BEAUNE   This fine hospital for the aged, poor and sick, was founded in 1443 by Nicholas Rolin, a pious *parvenu* lawyer. Its beautiful old buildings, designed in the Flemish style, with high, steep roofs and an immense cobbled courtyard, provide the greatest tourist attraction of the Côte d'Or. The endowment consisted of a number of vineyards, and these have been added to by the posthumous generosity of a number of testators. The wines are generally well made, and no doubt it was this that originally caused them to be sold at a premium. Nowadays they fetch even higher prices, but not entirely for the same reason: there is the glamour of the name *Hospices de Beaune*, and the certainty that the wines will command a high price throughout the world. Of late the prices have been high almost to the extent of absurdity. Before the auction, there is a tasting of samples. The sale is then conducted by the old method of *à la chandelle* – by the candle. A short length of taper is lit, and the last bidder to make his offer before the flame flickers out gets the wine.

Apart from its value as a charity, the auction serves two useful purposes: it enables the merchants of the Côte d'Or to assess the merits of the vintage by a fairly comprehensive tasting, and it sets the level of prices for the rest of the year. Only in very bad years is the auction not held. The wines are made up in various *cuvées* as follows:

RED WINES

Communes	*Cuvées*
Aloxe-Corton	Charlotte Dumay
	Docteur Peste
Auxey-Duresses	Boillot
Beaune	Bétault
	Brunet
	Clos des Avaux
	Dames Hospitalières
	Estienne
	Guigone de Salins
	Nicolas Rolin
	Pierre Virely
	Rousseau-Deslandes
Meursault	Henri Gélicot
Monthélie	Jacques Lebelin
Pommard	Billerdet
	Dames de la Chariteé
Savigny	Arthur Girard
	Cyrot
Savigny-Vergelesses	de Bay-Peste
	Forneret
	Fouquerand
Volnay	Blondeau
	General Muteau
Volnay-Santenots	Gauvrain
	Jehan de Massol

WHITE WINES

Communes	*Cuvées*
Corton-Charlemagne	Francois de Salins
Meursault	Baudot
	Goureau
	Jehan Humblot
	Loppin
Meursault-Charmes	Albert Grivault
	de Bahèzre de Lanley

Many of the *cuvées* are named after the donors. Although the wines are undoubtedly authentic (though some are over-chaptalized), their fate is in the hands of those who buy them. Thanks to the high price and kudos they command, it is not unlikely that some of the less scrupulous merchants succumb to the temptation of 'stretching' them, for there is no control over the issue of labels. Others are bought by restaurateurs and small merchants whose bottling ability may not be above suspicion.

HUNGARIAN WINES Hungary grows one wine of great renown – tokay – and many other lesser wines of no particular quality but very agreeable and reasonably priced. Excellent though tokay is, though, it is not as fine as its reputation would suggest, as this is largely based on the legendary Imperial Tokay Essence which was reputed to revive the dying when all doctors failed. After the war and the revolution very little was made and none was exported to the West, so the few bottles that remained became great rarities and fetched astronomical prices at auction. In 1972, however, small quantities once more became available.

Tokay (or Tokai) takes its name from the *Tokaj-Hegyalja* wine growing district. It is a sweet white wine of unique and fascinating flavour, derived from the shrivelled, highly sweet *aszu* berries which, like the great sweet wines of France and Germany, are attacked by the 'noble rot'. These are picked separately from the rest and are placed in traditional wooden butts called *puttonys*. After pressing, the juice is added to that derived from the grapes of the normal picking and the wine is then fermented. It is labelled according to the quantity of *aszu* wine which is mixed in before the fermentation, thus a bottle labelled 'five puttonys' will have that quantity of *aszu* berries added – each puttony being about 10 per cent of the whole. With each measure of *aszu* the richness increases, and all grades are made from one to six puttonys, but in practice one and two puttonys are rare as the wine tends to dry out rapidly in bottle and is not commercially very acceptable, while that of six puttonys is also rarely made, being both too rich and too expensive. The number of puttonys, however, is by no means the only criterion. As with all sweet wines, much depends on the vintage, and a three puttony wine of a fine vintage may be as rich as a five puttony wine of a lesser one. Once in bottle, it lasts almost indefinitely and wines have been tasted after two or three hundred years. Unlike most sweet white wines, tokay tastes best at room temperature.

The ancient tokay essence was made of *aszu* berries that were not pressed at all; the essence was released simply by the weight of the grapes themselves, and it was so full of sugar that its fermentation was inhibited, so that it was intense in flavour and sweetness, but not strong alcoholically. This is then added and a five or six puttonys aszu.

The least of the tokays is tokay szamorondni – literally 'tokay as it has grown'. To make this the aszu berries are not separated, and the quality is therefore very much more a matter of speculation. In the best years it approximates to the aszu in quality, but in lesser ones it is dry and not particularly notable.

Next most famous of the Hungarian wines is the Bulls' Blood of Eger (Egri bikavér). Its name suggests a manly sort of wine, and it lives up to its name. On the whole I prefer to drink it in the vigour of youth before it has been too long in bottle. Of the other districts, one of the most notable is around Lake Balaton, which is particularly famous for its Riesling wines, though excellent wines are also produced from the Furmint grape, while Somló, near the head of the lake, grows a Furmint of very distinctive character that takes an exceptionally long time to mature.

ICE. Ice is now essential to the barman and very nearly so to the wine waiter. For use in the bar, it should be chipped into relatively small pieces and shaken vigorously in the cocktail shaker. The cocktail is then poured out through the filter so that it is neatly chilled but is not in contact with the ice for long enough for the ice to become melted and to dilute the flavour too much (see COCKTAILS.) For the wine waiter, ice is synonymous with the ice bucket, though this device is wholly unnecessary in the home, where better results are generally achieved by slipping a bottle of white wine in the refrigerator for an hour or so before drinking (See TEMPERATURE.) Lumps of ice are sometimes also placed in wine, though such barbarous treatment is wholly inappropriate to any wine of quality, as it dilutes and spoils the flavour. A better arrangement is found in some of the Italian flasks which have ice compartments where ice – or an ice and salt freezing mixture – can be inserted to keep the wine cool without diluting it. The only wines that can properly have ice cubes put in them are those of extremely inferior ordinaire quality which can be diluted to taste with water or even soda water.

ICE WINE   See 'Eiswein' in GERMAN WINE TERMS.

INFERNO   See ITALIAN WINES.

IRANCY   See FRANCE, THE LESSER KNOWN WINES.

IRISH COFFEE   Sweet hot black coffee flavoured with Irish whiskey and topped with a layer of thick cream through which it is drunk. Similar drinks are now made using a variety of other spirits.

ISRAEL   The history of Israeli wine stretches back as far as the book of Genesis, but the wine trade in the modern sense is one of the most recent and dates only from the end of the last century. Its emergence as a notable potential exporter of wines is very much more recent. At first the Israeli wines were vinified in imitation of the great wines of Europe and unfortunately were often labelled with the names of the wines that they sought to imitate. Recently, however, Hebrew names have been generally adopted and this should give a chance for the wines to come into their own without the stigma of being imitations. The Israelis are undoubtedly making very great efforts in wine production and some of the wines are very promising, particularly the light white wines which have a delicacy that is remarkable in such a southern latitude. Generally speaking, the shippers do not market single vineyard wines, but produce blended wines, choosing the constituents from the various areas of the country so as to produce a product having the best possible balance. This would seem to be the ideal method, since it produces a consistent quality and a degree of balance which is seldom achieved in any single vineyard so far south.

ITALIAN WINES   For a wine lover, as for a lover of the arts, Italy is one of the most enchanting countries in Europe to travel around. It enjoys one great advantage: an immense range of soil and climate, from the cool, alpine climate of the north, to the parched, baked soils of the centre and south. It is perhaps surprising that from all these areas no truly great wine, comparable to the finest of France and Germany, has yet emerged. Perhaps it is a matter of temperament. At one extreme, the big companies produce their world-famous vermouths, while at the other peasants continue to grow and vinify their wines as they have for centuries – not very well! But all this is changing rapidly. The growers in the finest areas have already organized themselves, and these efforts are backed up by a much more rigorous wine law which will, it is hoped, get rid of some of the more doubtful practices and encourage the growing of quality wines. Not long ago, a much-publicized prosecution was started against a vendor of bogus chianti. This should put no one off Italian wines. There are rogues everywhere and in every trade, and it would do nothing but good if a bad wine merchant were occasionally shot to encourage the others.

Wines are marketed both under the names of the towns around which they are grown and under the names of grape varieties. Sometimes these are confusing; for instance Barbaresco is a village and Barbera a vine, which happens not to be grown there. Generally speaking geographical names are applied to wines grown in defined areas which enjoy some form of legal protection, whereas those sold under grape names may come from a rather vague area. The latter are quite often as good as the former but rarely, if ever, better. The vintage does not matter much and it is often not even indicated. There is not much difference on Mediterranean latitudes between the sunshine of one year and another, so that the wines are more consistent than those grown further north, and where a vintage is given, it indicates the age rather than the quality.

The number of different kinds of wine grown in Italy is bewildering. Piedmont grows some of the best. Many of these may fairly be compared with Rhône wines, which grow on much the same latitude. Barbaresco, for instance, is ruby red, dry, and has a delicate aroma. Barolo, its near neighbour, and vinified from the same Nebbiolo grapes, is a strongly flavoured red wine that is greatly improved by a few years in bottle. Nebbiolo is a red wine named after that most aristocratic of the Piedmont grape varieties, and it comes in three distinct styles: one is fairly dry but sparkling, a second is still and quite sweet, while the third is still, pretty dry, and rather aromatic. The last is generally thought best. Freisa is a light red wine, sometimes sweet and slightly sparkling. Gattinara (the best of which is sold as Gattinara Classico) is a good red wine. By far the most famous wine of this area, though, is asti spumante, a sparkling wine made principally from Muscat grapes. Being rather on the sweet side, it tends to be sneered at in this country, but is excellent, for instance, to drink with the Christmas pudding.

Visitors to Liguria – and they are many, for this includes the Italian Riviera – can enjoy a variety of local wines but the best known is the white cinqueterre, which may be anything from fairly dry to very sweet. It is well worth looking for, but beware of imitations.

Of the Lombardy wines, sassella is a good red; perversely, although sassella is also the name of a grape variety, most of the wine is vinified from the Nebbiolo. Inferno is a powerful red

ITALY

wine with far more charm than its name might suggest; while grumello is a red wine with a touch of sweet in it.

Trentino and the region of the Alto Adige, with its Alpine climate, grows some wines of real delicacy, often from vines that are more familiar in the north, such as the Sylvaner and the Traminer. These wines will be familiar to the many holiday makers who stay in Venice, as are those of the province of Veneto, which grows many interesting wines, especially around Verona. The best known of these is soave – a dry white wine, lightly flavoured, and almost as delightful as its name. The best red wines – and fhey are very good – are bardolino, valpolicella and valpatena. In Friuli and in the region of Venice pleasant, light red and white wines are grown, often sold under varietal names such as Riesling and Tocai (which has no connection with the Hungarian Tokay). The white wines are the most agreeable and though some good red wines are sold under the varietal names of Cabernet, Merlot, and Gamay.

Emilia and Romagna produce wines in great quantities but of little interest, which is odd in an area renowned for its food.

1 PIEDMONT: Asti Spumante, Moscati d'Asti Spumante, Barbaresco, Barbera d'Alba, Barbera d'Asti, Barbera del Monferrato, Barolo, Boca, Brachetto d'Acqui, Carema, Caluso Passito, Erbaluce di Caluso, Fara, Gattinara, Ghemme, Malvasia di Casorzo d'Asti, Nebbiolo d'Alba, Rubino di Cantavenna, Sizzano. 2 LOMBARDY: Botticino, Cellatica, Franciacorta Pinot, Franciacorta Rosso, Lugana, Oltrepò Pavese, Riviera del Garda Chiaretto, Riviera del Garda Rosso, Tocai di San Martino della Battaglia, Valtellina. 3 TRENTINO-ALTO ADIGE: Lago di Caldaro. 4 VENETO: Bardolino, Breganze, Colli Euganei, Gambellara, Prosecco di Conegliano-Valdobbiadene, Soave, Recioto di Soave, Valpolicella, Reciota della Valpolicella. 5 FRIULI-VENEZIA GIULIA: Collio Goriziano, Colli Orientali del Friuli, Grave del Friuli. 6 EMILIA-ROMAGNA: Albana di Romagna, Gutturnio dei Colli Piacentini, Lambrusco Grasparossa di Castelvetro, Lambrusco Salamino di S.Croce, Lambrusco di Sorbara, Sangiovese di Romagna. 7 TUSCANY: Bianco di Pitigliano, Brunello di Montalcino, Chianti, Elba Bianco, Elba Rosso, Montecarlo Bianco, Rosso delle Colline Lucchesi, Vernaccia di San Gimignano, Vino Nobile di Montepulciano. 8 MARCHE: Bianchello del Metauro, Rosso Conero, Rosso Piceno, Verdicchio dei Castelli di Jesi, Verdicchio di Matelica. 9 UMBIRA: Torgiano. 10 ABRUZZO: Montepulciano d'Abruzzo. 11 LAZIO: Colli Albani, Est! Est!! Est!!! di Montefiascone, Frascati, Marino, Trebiano di Aprilia, Merlot di Aprilia, Sangiovese di Aprilia. 12 CAMPANIA: Greco di Tufo, Ischia Bianco, Ischia Rosso, Taurasi. 13 PUGLIA: Locorotondo, Martina, San Severo. 14 CALABRIA: Cirò. 15 SICILY: Corvo, Etna, Marsala. 16 SARDINIA: Vermentino, Moscato, Malvasia, Vernaccia.

But Tuscany grows the most famous of all Italian wines: Chianti. Although white wines are sometimes grown in the same vineyards, only the reds may be sold as Chianti, which is an excellent table wine; but only too often those sold for export have been blended with coarser wines from the south. The best Chianti is Chianti Classico, distinguished by a label showing a black cockerel on a gold ground; it is grown in a delimited area and is matured for three years in the wood before bottling. On the whole, Chianti should be drunk young, for with age it tends to wither rather than mellow, and only too often in England it is frankly stale. The *fiaschi*, by the way, in which it is often sold, hold a litre, so although they cost more than the same wine in bottles, you get more for your money – though generally not that much more. If a Chianti is vinified for ageing, it is generally in a claret-shaped bottle rather than a flask. Although less well known than Chianti, Brunello di Montalcino is a greater wine – a wine of enormous flavour that needs to be matured for five or six years in cask and then for at least ten years in bottle before it is ready for drinking. Perhaps the nearest thing to it in France is the black wine of Cahors, though others have compared it with hermitage. The best white wines of the area are Montecarlo (which may also be red) and Vernaccia di San Gimignano. Vino santo, which is grown in Tuscany and in other parts of Italy, is especially prepared, attractive, very sweet to dessert wine.

Umbria's most famous wine is the white Orvieto, which can be dry but which is usually rather sweet. Like many Italian wines, it comes in various degrees of sweetness, and the sweeter version, sold as *abboccato* or *amabile* is the older established, the dry kind being a relatively new thing. The Orvieto flask holds three-quarters of a litre, not a litre.

Travelling into the Marches, the most distinguished wine is the fairly dry, austere, white Verdicchio dei Castelli di Jesi the wine that Hannibal's army is said to have become drunk on, a fate doubtless subsequently shared by many pilgrims to Rome. It is usually sold in horrible, fancy bottles. The province of Lazio grows the famous white frascati, a wine that can be anything from quite dry to very sweet. Quite why its name is so familiar is a bit of a mystery. The wine is good, and of a beautiful, golden colour, but not so good as all that. Perhaps its name evokes the vanished splendour of its namesake the

Edwardian restaurant, or perhaps the beauty of the town near
where it is grown – a town so close to Rome and yet so individual.
To every gastronome its name means something more than the
wine, yet one feels that the wine would make the name familiar
without any help from outside. Est! est!! est!!! is even more
famous. It is grown in two quite distinct styles, the one being
pale in colour and relatively dry while the other is golden and
sweet. The story of how it got its name has often been told: how
a bishop on his way to Rome sent his servant on ahead to write
'est!' (meaning *vinum bonum est*) on the door of any inn with
good wine. At Montefiascone the servant's enthusiasm so ran
away with him that the word appeared three times on one door,
and the bishop got no further, drinking himself contentedly into
his grave.

Some of the best white wines of every degree of sweetness
are grown in the large area of some fifty square miles known as
Castelli Romani in the Alban hills. The best of the vini dei
Castelli Romani also often have village or brand names, and red
wines, both dry and sweet, are also grown there, but they too are
normally sold under local or brand names. Red wines include
the agreeable, if very slight, cecubo, which scarcely lives up to
its ancient reputation. A local white falernium, or falerno, dis-
putes with the falernos of Campania the honour of being the
classic falernian, but is even less distinguished.

In Campania the red and white falernos also echo the name of
the classic falernian but with none of its renown. Around Naples,
the most famous wines are the white lacrima Christis, which have
many enthusiastic admirers, though others consider them to be
over-rated. The name is so attractive that it is exploited commercially by using it on wines that are fairly near misses geographically and nowhere near the target as regards flavour.

The red, pink and white wines of Capri also enjoy a certain
reputation but rather too many of them are said to come from
the mainland, while the vast coarse wines of Apulia are notable
for quantity rather than for quality. In Calabria the wines are
also noted for their sturdiness rather than for their finesse.

Of the Sicilian wines, the best known, and perhaps the least
typical, is marsala (which see). Many of the table wines grown
there are unexpectedly delicate for so southerly a latitude. The
locals go so far as to liken their red Corvo di Casteldaccia

(a very pleasant wine) to claret, but no Frenchman would agree with them. Good white corvos are also grown.

The other great island, Sardinia, is a law unto itself. Far off the mainland, it is as different as it is remote. Many travellers regard it as positively un-Italian. Its wines are certainly different. For one thing, the table wines tend to be one shade darker: white wines are *gris*, pink wines are red, and red wines are positively black. They also tend to be several degrees stronger than those of the mainland. The most distinctive wines of all, though are the aperitif wines which are often likened to sherry: Vernaccia is the best and most famous, but there are others such as Torbato di Alghero.

There are really two ways to taste and enjoy the great variety of Italian wines. Perhaps the best is to travel around the country, stopping at the *trattorias* to taste the local wine as you go along. The easiest and laziest is to visit the great Enoteca at Siena, where wines from all over Italy are available for tasting.

IZARRA   See LIQUEUR.

JOHANNISBERG   See RHINE.

JULEP   A long iced drink made with spirits and now particularly popular in America, though originating in England where it was known in the seventeenth century. There are many different recipes and strong views are held as to the correct formulation, particularly in the American south. One of the best known forms of julep is a mint julep. To make a version of this, a few small sprigs of mint should be twisted between the fingers to release the juices and dropped into a glass, and a small amount of sugar or sugar syrup is added – the equivalent of about a lump. This is covered with whisky and allowed to macerate for up to a quarter of an hour. The glass is then filled with finely crushed ice, and whisky to the top, and is stirred.

JULIÉNAS   See BURGUNDY.

JURA   See FRANCE, THE LESSER KNOWN WINES.

JURANÇON   See FRANCE, THE LESSER KNOWN WINES.

KIRSCH (KIRSCHWASSER)   See LIQUEUR.

KLOSTER EBERBACH   A monastery on the Rheingau, formerly the property of the Cistercian Order, who created a great vineyard there: the Steinberg. It is now the property of the German state.

KREUZNACH   See RHINE.

KÜMMEL   See LIQUEUR.

LAGER   See BEER.

LACHRIMA CHRISTI   See ITALIAN WINES.

LANGUEDOC   See FRANCE, THE LESSER KNOWN WINES.

LEES   The dregs at the bottom of a cask.

LIEBFRAUMILCH   See GERMAN WINE TERMS.

LIQUEUR   A liqueur is any sweetened and flavoured alcoholic drink, but the term is usually used to indicate a drink intended for after the meal – hence the French *digestif*. Many liqueurs do appear to have digestive qualities, particularly those compounded of herbs, and a considerable number were originally devised for medicinal purposes, including some of the famous monastic liqueurs. In the United States, liqueurs are known as *cordials*. The term *liqueur* is also used, perhaps somewhat loosely, in connection with old mature brandies and whiskies suitable for drinking neat after meals. The available range of liqueurs is enormous – indeed bewildering – and good examples are made in practically every country. Since these drinks are made of many different things, there is one good test of quality: the homogeneity of flavour. A liqueur should have a taste of its own and not appear to be a mixture of many different tastes. All the most famous liqueurs pass this test with flying colours. Any kind of spirit may be used, and the flavouring agents consist of herbs, such as peppermint, tarragon, thyme, and wormwood; wood barks, such as aloe and cinnamon; roots such as angelica, cloves, ginger, and liquorice; flowers such as camomile, lavender, and saffron; seeds, such as angelica seeds, aniseed, caraway, cocoa, and nutmeg; all manner of fruits; sugar and honey. The main ways of getting the flavours are by *maceration* or *infusion*, when the spirit soaks out the flavour from the natural product; *digestion*, which is maceration but using warmed alcohol; *percolation*, which is much the same process as a coffee percolator but using spirit; and *distillation*. The final processes are *compounding*, when flavouring agents obtained by any of the methods mentioned are mixed and blended together; a very highly skilled operation. Finally the liqueur has to be matured for a time in order to allow the various flavours to settle down in complete unity before bottling.

Of the fruit liqueurs the best known are cherry brandies (of which there are a wide variety), Maraschino (made from distilled cherries), apricot brandy and peach brandy. Citrus fruits provide the basis of a particularly popular range of liqueurs including Curaçao, Cointreau, and Grand Marnier, all flavoured with oranges; Van Der Hum, flavoured with naartjies, as well as with herbal flavours; and Forbidden Fruit, flavoured with shaddock.

The true fruit brandies, or *eaux-de-vie* (waters of life) are brandies distilled from fermented fruit juices rather than grape brandies flavoured with fruits. Calvados, or applejack, is distilled from apples; Kirsch, from cherries; Mirabelle, from mirabelle plums; Framboise, from raspberries. These are not really liqueurs at all.

The herbs used in making the various herbal liqueurs are legion, and what they consist of is invariably a closely kept secret. These liqueurs are amongst the finest *digestifs* and may be based on brandy or whisky. Of the brandy liqueurs the best known are Bénédictine, Chartreuse, La Vieille Cure, Izarra, and Strega. Those based on whisky include Drambuie and Glen Mist. All these provide highly complex flavours derived from many herbs, but in addition there are a number of liqueurs in which the flavour of a single herb predominates. Aniseed, for example, provides the principal flavouring in Pernod, Anisette, and Anis Del Mono. Caraway seeds flavour Kümmel. Both these flavourings together with gold flakes are found in the famous and exotic Danzig Goldwasser. Peppermint provides the flavour for Crème de Menthe.

Chocolate is used as the flavouring in Crème de Cacao, while the recently introduced Royal Mint Chocolate Liqueur combines the flavour of mint with that of chocolate. Coffee is used as the flavouring for Tia Maria.

Advocaat does not fall into any of the above categories. It is thick, yellow, and creamy, made from egg yolks and a brandy. A number of makes are available all of which differ in the flavouring agents that are added.

A glass of a good liqueur perfectly rounds off a meal. And the expense need not be great: most liqueurs last very well after the bottle has been broached, and few people would take more than a very small measure. Liqueurs should preferably be served in smal tulip shaped glasses, so that the excellent aroma, which is one of their great attractions, can be properly appreciated. Only too often hotels serve them in tall narrow glasses which open up at the top and are narrowest in the middle, so that half the effect is immediately lost. The scent is further enhanced by gently warming the glass in the palm of the hand. As an alternative, particularly after lunch on a hot summer's day, some liqueurs taste very well drunk 'on the rocks' – that is to say in a larger glass with pieces of ice in. Cointreau and Crème de Menthe can both be very attractive drunk in this way.

Some sweet, fortified wines are sold in France as *vins de liqueur*. They are suitably drunk with a sweet pudding or on their own, in place of a liqueur after a meal.

LIQUOREUX   An adjective applied to sweet dessert wines.

LILLET   See APERITIF.

LOIRE   The wide valley of the Loire is one of the most peaceful and beautiful in Europe. Famous for its châteaux, the countryside that surrounds it is gentle and utterly charming. Its wines follow the same pattern. The Loire is the longest river in France, and it is not surprising that an immense variety of wines grow in its valley.

The famous wines of the upper Loire are sancerre on the left bank and pouilly fumé on the right. Both are delicious: dry, white, and with considerable natural acidity which gives them great freshness. Further down stream, and entering the region of the châteaux, the Touraine grows red, white, and rosé wines that are generally light in alcohol. The white wines of Vouvray and Montlouis are amongst the best, while the finest red wines are those of Chinon and Bourgueil. A certain amount of pétillant wine is also grown. Further down river, Anjou is especially famous for its vin rosé de Cabernet, while the white wines of the Coteaux du Layon are amongst the best sweet white dessert wines of France. Saumur is famous for its delicate white sparkling wine and also grows excellent still white wines. Finally, before the river reaches its estuary, on either side of the town of Nantes, comes the Muscadet region, growing some of the freshest, most delightful, and most famous white wines of the whole of the Loire.

Loire wines are excellent to drink in this country, but the lightest and most delicate of them do not travel very well, especially in cask, and they are even better when drunk on the spot, while in this country it is often worth while to pay the extra for French bottling. The dry white wines are good as aperitifs or with fish, especially shell fish, while muscadet is becoming very popular with oyster lovers. The sweet white wines are not generally so sweet as those of Bordeaux, for instance, and taste best with a not too sweet pudding, such as a soufflé. The red wines, tending to be rather light, are ideal luncheon wines, or dinner wines on a summer's day. Many of the rosés, especially those of Anjou, are fairly sweet but not too assertively so; they can accompany almost anything and are ideal picnic wines, tasting good with the prawns yet sweet enough to stand up to the strawberries.

The Loire is a fine piece of countryside for the wine lover to travel in.

LUNEL   See FRANCE, THE LESSER KNOWN WINES.

LUTOMER   See YUGOSLAVIA.

LUXEMBOURG   Luxembourg is scarcely one of the great wine growing countries of the world, and most of its wine is consumed in the Duchy, though a little of it is now on sale in this country. Lying on the upper reaches of the Moselle, it is not surprising that the wines have something of a moselle character, but tend to be thinner and more acid. The best of them are very good indeed, delightfully fresh, but they are only to be found in Luxembourg itself. A certain amount of pleasant dry, white pétillant wine called *perlwein* is also produced and exported.

MÂCON   See BURGUNDY.

MADEIRA   'Have some madeira m'dear': Flanders and Swan have perhaps done as much for madeira as George Leybourne did for champagne when his song 'Champagne Charlie' swept London in 1869. And the image of madeira remains rather with 1869 – an image of moustacheoed and slightly lecherous Victorians. Like many other things that our great-grandfathers enjoyed, it went through a period of neglect, but now it is coming into its own again, and a very good thing too. The island of Madeira was discovered in 1419, and the first Englishman arrived 6 years later. The English have been there practically ever since, and most of them have devoted their attentions to making wine.

Compared with sherry and port, madeira certainly suffered something of an eclipse, but goodness only knows why: it is one of the greatest wines in the world and one of the most adaptable. The great wines of Madeira are named after the vines that give rise to them: malmsey, bual, verdelho, and sercial. (listed from sweetest to driest). All are fortified wines, but the two drier wines – sercial and verdelho – are vinified in much the same way as sherry, while the two sweeter ones are made in much the same way as port: the former are allowed to ferment completely and are then fortified with an addition of alcohol at a later stage, while the latter have little alcohol added before the fermentation so that the ferments are inhibited and a larger proportion of the natural sugar is retained. One process is unique to madeira: the *estufa*, when the wine is first gradually heated and then is equally slowly cooled again. No one knows quite how this process originated, but it may well be that the merchants found that wine shipped over the equator had a peculiar elegance and maturity all of its own, and tried to emulate the conditions that produced it.

Sercial is relatively light in colour and body, and is comparatively dry: it is principally an aperitif wine. Verdelho is deeper in colour and body, and is sweeter; it is a versatile wine and may be enjoyed before or after a meal. Bual is one stage deeper and sweeter; although some madeira lovers enjoy it as an aperitif, it is generally considered to be a dessert wine. Both the last two are, as it were, madeira drinkers' madeiras; they have special subtleties that intrigue as well as satisfy. But the most impressive madeira of all is malmsey: deep and gloriously sweet, the best examples are magnificent dessert wines. Apart from these, some of the blended wines are sold under old-established names like 'London Particular', but two names are so well established as to call for special comment: 'Southside' and 'Rainwater'. Both of these are found mostly in America – the former almost entirely so – but the latter is readily available in England. 'Southside' is a rich blend of the best wines grown on the southern slopes of the island.

'Rainwater' is a drier blend, mostly from the sercial grapes grown high on the hillsides where there is no irrigation, and where the vines have to rely on the rainfall for their water.

No other wine lives so long: in cask it rivals sherry and in bottle it excels port. Very old madeiras are necessarily expensive, but they are treasures worth seeking. Madeira has one characteristic in particular that is useful as compared with sherry. When opened it does not rapidly oxidize so a bottle can be left open for two or three weeks without deterioration. It should normally be served at room temperature.

MADERIZATION This is a phenomenon which occurs to most white wines if kept too long either in the barrel or subsequently in bottle. The wine becomes oxidized, turns brown in colour, and acquires a rather unpleasant bouquet which is generally considered to resemble that of the madeira – hence the name. In very sweet wines like a sauternes, it is often not particularly objectionable as the sweetness of the wine masks it, but in dry white wines it can be total ruin.

MAJORCA See SPANISH TABLE WINES.

MALAGA The wines of Malaga are now almost completely out of favour in this country, and very few are imported, but once it was otherwise. In Elizabethan days they were generally known here as *malligo sack*, and later as *mountain* – as any collector of wine labels knows.

A typical malaga is a strong, rich dessert wine not unlike a brown sherry. The strength, though, is natural, and there is no fortification. Those exported to this country are almost exclusively the cheaper grades, but despite their modest price, they are very pleasant. In Spain there is a far greater variety including some attractive very dry wines.

MALMSEY See MADEIRA.

MALTA The Maltese wine industry is rapidly expanding, but most of the wine is drunk locally and is not of any great quality, though some of the white wine, despite being very southern in character, has plenty of natural acidity and is well made.

MANZANILLA See SHERRY.

MARC A relatively cheap spirit distilled from fermented grape residues in the red wine areas (which includes champagne, as the majority of grapes used for making champagne are in fact red). Marc is distinctly an acquired taste – but like many tastes of this kind it appears to give especial pleasure to those who have acquired it. Given age in cask, some marcs can become quite distinguished, and perhaps the most famous of all are *marc de champagne* and *marc de bourgogne*.

MARCOBRUNN   See RHINE.

MARGAUX   See CLARET.

MARSALA   Although grown in Sicily, this wine is really an English creation, for it owes its origin and ancient popularity to the enterprise of John Woodhouse, who founded his business in 1773. His family had formerly lived in Portugal, and it may also be that he was familiar with Spain, for the method of making marsala has much in common with that used in sherry. The wine is fortified, and is often matured on the solera system (see SOLERA). Most marsalas are sweet dessert wines that are pleasant but have no particular distinction, though the best of them, especially if given time to mature in bottle, can be quite elegant. There are also some special kinds of marsala, such as *marsala all'nova* which is a wine combined with egg yolks to produce something half way between a dessert wine and a liquid pudding.

MARSANNAY   A village in Burgundy near Dijon which is especially noted for its dry, rosé wine.

MARTINI   See COCKTAILS.

MASTICHA   See GREEK WINE.

MAVRODAPHNE   See GREEK WINE.

MAXIMIN GRÜNHAUS   See MOSELLE.

MAY WINE   A spiced fruit cup made of Rhine wine.

MEAD   This is made by fermenting honey and water, and is one of the most ancient of all alcoholic drinks. It is also known as hydromel, while metheglin was a spiced mead whose name was derived from the Welsh *meddyglyn*. Although brewing and cider making flourish enormously in Britain, the making of mead is now little more than a cottage industry, though attempts are being made to revive it on a commercial scale.

MÉDOC See CLARET.

METHEGLIN OR METHAGLIN A spiced or medicated mead, originally Welsh.

MEURCUREY See BURGUNDY.

MEURSAULT See BURGUNDY.

MINERAL WATER This term originally applied to spa waters containing various minerals which were believed to be of medical value. It has now been corrupted into meaning any carbonated non-alcoholic drink. Genuine mineral waters still exist in a considerable quantity, however. Malvern water, for instance, is practically tasteless and is much favoured for diluting spirits. The slightly alkaline evian and vichy waters are particularly popular on the Continent to be drunk with meals and are said to aid digestion. Another popular water of this general kind is perrier, which is highly effervescent like soda water, and which makes an excellent drink taken by itself, chilled, with a slice of lemon in it.

MIRABELLE See LIQUEUR.

MITTELRHEIN See RHINE.

MOELLEUX The term used to indicate a sweet, fruity wine.

MONBAZILLAC See FRANCE, THE LESSER KNOWN WINES.

MONTECARLO See ITALIAN WINES.

MONTILLA-MORILES These wines are grown in Andalusia on soil similar to that of the sherry vineyards, using to some extent the same vines, and in much the same climate. It follows that the wine has a very distinct resemblance to sherry; indeed, in earlier times wines from this district were regularly sold as sherry. Perhaps the most popular of all kinds of sherry is that sold as *amontillado*; and the word quite simply means 'resembling the wines of Montilla'. So although the wines of Jerez are now more popular than those of Montilla, they continue to pay it a somewhat back-handed compliment.

Montilla-Moriles wines have considerable natural strength so they require no fortification, and they have a style and quality that is all their own. With age in cask they can attain grandeur, but those most readily available are the younger, fresh finos. Often marketed in hock-shaped bottles, they are excellent wines and are almost' invariably good value. They are best served as dry aperitif wines, alternatives to fino sherry.

MONTLOUIS See LOIRE.

MONTPELIER See FRANCE, THE LESSER KNOWN WINES.

MONTRACHET See BURGUNDY.

MOONSHINE An American term originally applied to illegally distilled spirits, particularly whisky, but now sometimes applied to legally distilled spirits of questionable quality.

MOREY-SAINT-DENIS See BURGUNDY.

MORGON See BURGUNDY.

MOROCCO Despite its Moslem religion, Morocco has a very substantial production of wine, most of it red with a little rosé and a smaller quantity of white. They tend to be big, unsubtle things as one would expect from the hot climate.

MOSELBLÜMCHEN See GERMAN WINE TERMS.

MOSELLE (In German, Mosel). The German vineyards are the most northerly of all the great vineyards of Europe, and the moselle vineyards are the most northerly of all. One would therefore expect a rather acid, delicate white wine, and indeed moselle is both those things, but one would perhaps not expect, in a wine grown so far north, such fruitiness. The wines of the moselle are undoubtedly superlative, and if they were not, they would almost certainly not be grown at all; for viticulture so far north is hazardous and difficult. In the valley of the Moselle it is particularly difficult because of the precipitous slopes. It is these slopes, with their slate soil, that give the wine its quality and the vines their exposure to the sun; scenically, the valley is one of the most beautiful of all great wine growing districts.

The great vine is the riesling, and the finest vineyards are those of the middle moselle, stretching roughly from Piesport to Erden. Perhaps the most famous village of all is Bernkastel with its supremely great Bernkasteler Doktor vineyard. Magnificent wines are grown, though, in several of its neighbours, notably Piesport, Graach, Wehlen, and Zeltingen; each of these village names has the suffix 'er' added to it when used descriptively on a wine label. Other great wines are grown on the banks of the tributaries of the Moselle, the Saar and Ruwer. Those of the former valley are often described as 'steely', and certainly in the poorer years this hard, almost metallic taste used to give them an austerity which only their most devoted admirers could tolerate, though this has been considerably mitigated by modern cellar techniques. The Saar wines are always exceptionally light, and in the finest years this gives them a unique elegance. The most famous centres are Wiltingen, and Ayl. The Ruwer (pronounced Roover) is the smallest of the Moselle's tributaries – a busy stream rather than a river – and the wines grown on its banks vie with those of the Saar in delicacy; if anything they are even more delicate. Production is very small and the most famous wines come from the Maximin Grünhaus.

So fresh and so good, a young moselle is a perfect aperitif, especially if it has that rare characteristic *spritizig*: an almost imperceptible touch of effervescence which tickles the tongue. They are also particularly good to drink with fish but, despite being so delicate, they are so assertive that they go surprisingly well with meatier dishes which one would expect to be alien to them. Although the majority of moselles are comparatively dry, the sweetness increases as one passes from spätlese to auslese to beerenauslese to trockenbeerenauslese (see GERMAN WINE TERMS.). The latter two qualities frequently produce wines of great sweetness, and quite outstanding elegance. They are so supremely good, that in my view they should not be drunk with any food, but alone, after a meal. All moselle wines should be served chilled.

MOULIN-À-VENT   See BURGUNDY.

MOULIS   See CLARET.

MOUNTAIN   See MALAGA.

MOUSSEUX   French term meaning sparkling wine.

MULLED DRINKS   These are particularly suitable for our climate and yet seem to have gone quite out of favour – perhaps because they take some trouble to make. They are well worth making, though, especially on a bitterly cold winter's evening. The basis of mulled wine is simply wine heated (though not boiled) with spices, sugar, and sometimes a little water added to taste. The wine must be mulled in a saucepan which will not give it an extraneous flavour. Aluminium vessels are fatal, enamelled ones (very carefully cleaned out) possible, earthenware better still, and silver ideal, as well as being impressive. A few fortunate families still have Victorian mulling kettles with spirit lamps underneath. Claret mulls very well, but burgundy does not; and this appears to apply equally to the imitations of those wines. So either choose a light dry table wine or the other extreme, port or sherry. The following recipes are taken from a little book by William Terrington with the improbable name *Cooling Cups and Dainty Drinks* published in 1869.

To Mull Wine. Into a clean stewpan pour 1 pint of water; add ½ oz. bruised ginger, cinnamon, cloves, nutmeg, the spices most likely to predominate: cover up, and boil down to ½ pint of water; then strain clear, and add ¼ lb. of sugar and 1 pint of claret.

Many of the mulled drinks have ecclesiastical names ranging from beadle to pope by way of archbishop and cardinal. Perhaps the best of these, as well as the best known, is *Bishop*, which is simply mulled port. In the simplest version, a bottle of ruby port is warmed with half a bottle of water, half an orange with cloves stuck in it, and a little sugar. When the mixture is hot, a match should be applied to the steam, which will burn with a splendidly infernal colour. As soon as this happens, the flame should be put out by pouring the Bishop into a bowl and it should be drunk hot. But Terrington had a more complicated formula to which he gave a name calculated to horrify the church authorities:

A Good Bishop. Stick a good lemon full of cloves, which roast before the fire till it becomes a rich dark brown; meanwhile pound together ½ lb. loaf-sugar, a little grated nutmeg, ginger, cinnamon, 2 cloves, 1 allspice, the thin rind of a lemon; place this mixture when well incorporated, in a bowl by the side of the fire, adding ½ pint of water, ½ pint of port wine (or roussillon), 1 bottle of claret; strain all through muslin; heat the mixture, but do not let it burn, and into the empty warm bowl drop in the lemon; give it a press with the spoon; add a wine-glass of cherry brandy, and the mixture; keep it hot, and you will find this a really good bishop.

N.B. This bishop can be made the day previous, and mulled when required for use.

Cardinal. Cut 3 tangerine oranges in slices, add $\frac{1}{4}$ oz. bruised cinnamon (or 3 drops essence of cinnamon), a little mace, 3 drops essence of nutmeg, 3 bruised cardamom seeds, and 4oz. of dissolved barley-sugar in 1 pint of hot water; cover, and let the mixture simmer for half an hour; strain clear with pressure; add 1 quart of Rhenish wine, which warm up; if too highly flavoured, add more wine.

Negus. Quart of boiling water, pint of port (or roussillon) wine $\frac{1}{2}$ lb. loaf-sugar, juice and zest of a lemon, juice of 2 oranges, little powdered cinnamon and nutmeg to taste; mix when cool; strain, and serve warm; sherry or any other wine can be substituted for the port, but port-wine negus is usually made.

MUSCADET   See LOIRE.

MUSCATEL   The Muscatel (or moscatel) vine is one of the most long established recorded in the history of viticulture, certainly dating back to Roman times. It takes its name from a tendency to attract flies. The grapes produced are extremely sweet and have a characteristic aroma, which is imparted to the wine. The grape is also unusual in being at home over a very wide range of climatic conditions and soils, so that muscatel wines are grown in most wine growing countries, and are generally very rich dessert wines of considerable character.

MUSIGNY   See BURGUNDY.

MUST   Grape juice before fermentation is complete.

NACKENHEIM   See RHINE.

NAHE   The Nahe is a tributary of the Rhine joining it at Bingen. It runs its course roughly parallel to the Moselle and although its wines have an individuality of their own, ma ·y of them subtly combine the features both of the Moselle and of the Rhine. On the upper reaches of the river, in particular there is a certain amount of slate in the soil, and the wines are particularly like those of the Moselle, while further down ey are closer in style to hocks. The wine-growing area is cer red round Kreuznach, though the best known name is Schloss Böckelheim. Because the wines of the Nahe are perhaps less well-known than the great names of hock and moselle, the prices are sometimes more attractive, and the wines themselves could hardly be more attractive.

NAPA   See AMERICA.

NAPOLEON BRANDY   A name given to certain brandies to indicate great age, but these brandies have absolutely no connection whatsoever with Napoleon. Any brandy bottled during the Napoleonic time would deteriorate rather than improve in bottle, while any brandy left in cask for that length of time would be altogether too woody and thoroughly unpleasant.

NECTAR   The wine of the Greek gods.

NEGUS   See MULLED DRINKS.

NIERSTEIN   See RHINE.

'NOBLE ROT'   Noble rot is the ultimate stage in the development of the grape, when it is over-ripe, and is attached by a fungus called *botrytis cinerea*. This kind of attack is a highly beneficial one, and it only occurs in certain vineyard areas: those producing the finest quality sweet wines. When the fungus attacks a grape, it shrinks, loosing water, and gaining proportionally in the concentration of sugar and flavour. The yield of wine is low, but the quality is exceptionally good, and hence the price tends to be high, though not as high as it ought to be simply because sweet wines are unfashionable. Without this admirable fungus it would be impossible to make the great sweet wines of Sauternes and Barsac, or the incomparable beerenauslese and trockenbeerenauslese wines of Germany – to mention only the greatest.

NOG   A mixed drink containing egg, such as a mixture of egg and brandy.

NORTH AFRICA   North African vineyards are near the southern limit of viticulture in the northern hemisphere; and indeed many would say that they are too near the limit, for wines grown on the southern shores of the Mediterranean tend to be notable for their vigour rather than their finesse, and many of them are frankly just 'plonk'. Some are so coarse that they are not even good plonk, and they earned a reputation worse than they deserved by rather indiscriminate buying of the Algerian wines which were imported into this country just after the war. Although no really great wines are grown in North Africa, the best are very agreeable, particularly some that are now being imported from Tunisia. See also MOROCCO.

NUITS ST GEORGES   See BURGUNDY.

OEIL DE PERDIX   Literally 'partridge eye' – a rosé of a light tawny colour.

OENOLOGY   See ENOLOGY.

OESTRICH   See THE RHINE.

OIDIUM   A fungus disease of the vine, otherwise known as *oidium tuckeri* or powdery mildew, or more precisely, as *uncinula necator* or *uncinula spiralis*. Indigenous to North America, it was brought over to Europe on vines in the nineteenth century, when it caused considerable devastation. It remains a permanent menace but is now fully controlled by spraying.

OLOROSO   See SHERRY.

OPPENHEIM   See RHINE.

ORDINAIRE   *Vin ordinaire* is the common wine of France, mostly grown in the south, and formerly imported on a large scale from Algeria.

ORVIETO   See ITALIAN WINES.

OUZO   See GREEK WINE.

PAARL   See SOUTH AFRICA.

PAILLE   Literally 'straw'. In the past wines were made by letting the grapes dry on straw mats and, after drying, being pressed and fermented to produce luscious wines. Such wines are still made in France and Spain.

PALATINATE   See THE RHINE.

PALESTINE   See ISRAEL.

PALETTE   See FRANCE, THE LESSER KNOWN WINES.

PALO CORTADO   See SHERRY.

PASSE-TOUS-GRAINS   A red wine of little quality made in Burgundy from a mixture of Pinot and Gamay grapes.

PASTEURIZATION A process of heating wines or other liquids, such as milk, sufficiently to kill any ferments etc., which may be in them, but not so hot as wholly to spoil the flavour. A wine so treated is safe in that it is not likely to change much, and many bad wines have been saved by it, but no wine so treated will never mature to perfection.

PASTIS An aniseed and herb flavoured aperitif originating around Marseilles. When water is poured in, it becomes dramatically cloudy. The best known brands are Pernod, and Ricard.

PATRAS See GREECE.

PAUILLAC See CLARET.

PEACH BRANDY See LIQUEUR.

PEDRO XIMIENEZ (P.X.) The name of a grape widely grown in the sherry country where it can produce either dry or sweet wines, but the varietal name is applied only to sweet wines which are specially vinified and generally used for blending, though a small quantity is sold for drinking rather in the manner of a liqueur.

PELURE D'OIGNON Literally 'onion skin'. A term with two meanings: it is generally applied to young rosé wines of a brownish tawny colour resembling an onion skin; it is also used to describe the browning colour which certain red wines acquire with age.

PERIGNON, DOM See CHAMPAGNE.

PERNOD See ABSINTHE and PASTIS.

PERRY A drink of the same general kind as cider, but made of pears instead of apples. Like cider, it is made either to be still or sparkling, and it is the latter kind which is particularly popular at the present time. One of the best known brands is Babycham.

PÉTILLANT Slightly sparkling.

PETITE CHAMPAGNE See COGNAC.

PFALZ See RHINE.

PHYLLOXERA Phylloxera is the worst of all the plagues that have attacked the vine, and it is still very much with us. The phylloxera is an insect – an aphid, generally known as *phylloxera vestatrix* (the devastating leaf-dryer), though several other scientific names have been given to it from time to time. Loosely, it is known as the 'vine louse'. It was first noticed in hothouses in England, but its real mischief was in the wine growing areas where it was imported on vines brought over from the United States of America in the hope that these would be resistant to the fungus disease of oidium (which see) which was at that time causing havoc in the European vineyards. Unfortunately, as often happens, the cure proved worse than the disease. It is a horrible looking insect (when looked at through a magnifying glass) and breeds at a horrifying rate. They form galls on the roots, which isolate the root from the plant and so starve it. The first printed report of an attack by the insect in France was written in 1867, and the disease spread with appalling rapidity. By 1880 it was practically everywhere in France and the other major wine growing countries of Europe, though it did not reach Greece until 1898 and has not yet reached Cyprus. At first various chemical remedies were tried in the hope of exterminating the insect, the most popular being carbon disulphide, but these proved only a very limited success, and the only real remedy was to graft the vines on to resistant roots imported from America. This in itself, however, involved great difficulties as it was no easy matter to find resistant roots which were at once compatible with the soil and with the native vine. The devastation was extremely serious and brought ruin on many growers.

The year 1880 is usually given as the dividing line between the pre-phylloxera and post-phylloxera wines in France, but this is really wildly inaccurate. The phylloxera was not a sudden phenomenon, but invaded and spread over a substantial period of time. Nor were vineyards necessarily grubbed up and replaced in a single operation, so one vineyard may well have been attacked in say 1875, and a near neighbour not replanted for twenty years. Some vineyards did not have to be replanted at all, as the insect finds great difficulty in penetrating sandy soil, so that it has left Colares in Portugal and some of the vineyards near Aigues Mortes in France clear to the present day. There is a small plantation of native vines at Quinta do Noval, producing fine port, a vineyard of native vines owned by Bollinger in the champagne district, and quite a number of native vines still left in Germany, particularly along the Moselle, which has slatey soil that the phylloxera finds it difficult to penetrate. No doubt the dispute will go on indefinitely as to whether the pre-phylloxera wines were better than the post-phylloxera. Certainly the wine grown in the Nacional part of the Quinto do Noval vineyard, from the native vines, appears to be consistently superior to that made from the grafted vines, but this may well be partly accounted for by the area of the vineyard in which the vines are grown. The truth probably is that, in most areas, there is not really very much difference between the two. Young vines tend to give poorer wines than old ones and this, coupled with a series of bad vintages in France at the beginning of this century, caused a degree of panic which was not justified by the facts. One good thing certainly resulted: many of the poorer quality vines and the poorer varieties, which flourished throughout even the major vineyards of Europe in the last century, were eliminated in favour of the best when the vineyards were replanted, and this has certainly done good for the overall quality of wine. Another thing is certain: that the pre-phylloxera clarets are not worth the astronomic and absurd prices which they regularly fetch nowadays in the sale rooms.

PIESPORT See MOSELLE.

PIMENT A spiced, honey-flavoured beverage made from wine or mead.

PIMM'S See CUPS.

PINEAU DES CHARENTES A fortified wine made in the Cognac area and used as an aperitif.

PIQUÉ Literally 'pricked': wine that has begun to turn into vinegar.

PLASTERING A process whereby plaster of Paris (gypsum) is added to the grapes when they are pressed in order to increase the acidity. It has long been the practice in the sherry area where it works well. It was the subject of considerable controversy during the nineteenth century, largely because it was not fully understood.

POMEROL See CLARET.

POMMARD   See BURGUNDY.

PORT   Port has long been described as the Englishman's wine though its connection with this country only goes back to the end of the seventeenth century, so that it is much more recent than bordeaux, and the French now drink more of it than we do. It is the British who largely created it, though, thanks to the politicians rather than the wine merchants; for in 1677 the importation of French wines were forbidden and, although the ban was easily circumvented, the penal duties remained throughout the eightenth century, following the Methuen Treaty of 1703 which provided for English cloths to be imported into Portugal and for Portuguese wine to be imported into England. The oldest existing port firm – Kopke & Co. – was founded by a German in 1638, but there followed a spate of British firms, many of them originally trading as general merchants, dealing particularly in dried cod from Newfoundland and English woollens. Warre & Co. date from 1670, Croft & Co. from 1678, Quarles Harris from 1680, Taylor, Fladgate & Yeatman, from 1692, Offley Forrester from 1729, Sandeman from 1790, Graham from 1814, and Cockburn from 1815, just to name some of the most famous firms who trade with this country. But although the French are now the largest drinkers of port taken as a whole, the British remain the largest drinkers of vintage port, the only other market worth mentioning for vintage port being the Scandinavian countries.

Port is grown in the Alto Douro, a carefully delineated area up the River Douro, beginning to the west of Regua and continuing eastwards up to the Spanish frontier, though the finest wines tend to be grown in roughly the middle of that area. Both red and white wines are grown though the trade is predominantly in reds, which are vinified by a method unique to port. In the traditional method the grapes were first separated from their stalks, and then loaded into square granite wine presses or *lagars*, about two feet deep. The grapes were then pressed by foot, mostly by men but sometimes with women as well, working as many as seventeen in a single *lagar*. The soft human foot (well washed beforehand) acts as a perfect pressing tool, crushing the grapes while leaving the pips intact. The must begins to ferment in the *lagar* and slowly gathers colour from the skin of the grapes. When it is sufficiently coloured, it is run off into

106

casks which already contain a certain amount of alcohol. This suppresses the fermentation before all the sugar has been used up, and so results in a relatively sweet wine. White port was made in the same way but using white grapes and, to keep the wine as light in colour as possible, the treading is reduced to a minimum. That, at any rate, was the picturesque traditional method, but it called for a great deal of labour which is just not available nowadays. It was getting scarce as early as 1960 and experimental installations were at work using the Ducellier system of fermentation, in which the grapes are passed into concrete vats and the gas produced by the fermentation is used to bring about a continuous circulation of the must, resulting in even better contact with the grape skins than in the traditional system, and consequently providing very high quality wine. It is less picturesque, but every bit as good, and without it the port trade would have died. It is now used by most of the big shippers.

Once the port has been fermented, it is allowed to mature initially in oak casks. As it matures, it becomes steadily more mellow to the taste and lighter in colour. Wines that are matured in the wood until they are ready to drink are known as *wood ports*, and the great majority are matured in this way. At a relatively early stage of the maturation, when the colour is still deep, the ports are known as *ruby*. As they grow old in cask, and the colour gets steadily lighter, they are known as *tawny*, and a genuine, very old tawny port is a real port drinker's port – a connoisseur's delight. But simply because it has had to spend so long in cask, it is necessarily expensive. Cheap tawny ports are never quite what they purport to be, being blended with a mixture of ruby port and white port, to make the price right. In practice, all wood ports are blended from wines derived from a number of years, so that the younger wines in a fine blend give vigour, while the older ones give delicacy, a combination providing a perfect balance.

The other way to mature port is in bottle. Vintage port is wine of a single year which is bottled when it is only two or at the most three years old, so that almost all its maturing goes on inside the bottle. This takes a very great deal longer than in the wood, and the wine normally has to be kept for at least fifteen years before it tastes anything like it should – and a fine vintage should be kept a good deal longer. Most vintages taste at their best after about a quarter of a century, but some take longer still, and the finest can last over fifty years before they begin to fade. A vintage port needs to mature undisturbed so that the very heavy sediment which it throws collects around the bottle, forming a crust which remains in the bottle when the wine is decanted – as it must be. A really well matured vintage port has practically no deposit apart from the crust, and the best way of decanting it is with the aid of a silver port funnel, which collects the large pieces of crust and gives a reflection so that any small deposit which may be coming over can be seen immediately and the decanting stopped in time, as the bottles are often so dark and encrusted, both inside and out, that the usual way of shining a light through is impracticable.

In between come *crusted* ports (or *crusting* ports) and *late bottled vintage* ports. The former are fine ports which have long been popular in this country, and are blends made of relatively young wines and intended for maturing in the bottle, so that they are bottled when their average age is five or six years old, giving them a good start as compared with the vintage ports, and then continue the maturation in bottle so that they nevertheless have much of a vintage port's character, while being ready to drink much sooner. Late bottled vintage port (a term which has been so abused that it has become distinctly unpopular with the Portuguese authorities) is a wine of a single vintage, kept in cask for six or seven years, and then bottled. One of the difficulties with this term is that such wines tend to be sold as vintage ports, which they most emphatically are not. A vintage port *must* be bottled after two or at most three years and have its maturation in the bottle and not in the cask. 'Late bottled vintage ports' therefore tend to give unscrupulous or ignorant traders weapons for fraud. Taken as wines in their own right, and treated as what they are – a variant on wood ports – they can be admirable.

White port is intended as an aperitif and should be served as that, well chilled. The French also drink red port – usually cheap tawny – chilled as an aperitif, though it is a taste which few other countries share. Traditionally port should be red, and drunk after the meal. It is excellent with cheese, but perhaps even better with nuts and dried fruit. It also goes extremely well with an apple. The existence of vintage port may be regarded as one of the few compensations for the English winter, as vintage port tastes much at its best in bitterly cold weather. It should be avoided on hot days, especially for lunch, and is rarely drunk in Portugal.

PORTER A form of brown ale popular in the nineteenth century but now extinct.

PORTUGUESE TABLE WINES Portugal is one of the most delightful of all wine countries to travel through, tasting as you go. It is full of pleasant surprises and the wines are generally well made. They are grown throughout the country from north to south and from east to west, so it is not surprising that they exist in bewildering variety. The most important areas, however, are the areas of the Vinhos Verdes in the north-west, the Dão, in the middle and about three-quarters of the way up, and a group of smaller areas round about Lisbon. The wine growers of all principal districts are subject to a *designacão do origem* system, comparable with the French *appellation controlée*. When buying one of these wines, there are two words that are worth looking out for, *reserva* and *garrafeira*. Both mean the same thing: selected wines matured in bottle. In practice, the former is generally used on wines with about four years bottle age, and the latter on wines with about eight years bottle age.

The vinhos verdes – red, pink and white – are grown in the enchanting and extraordinary vineyards of the Minho region, often unkempt on trees or growing on pergolas around the perimeters of fields, with vegetables growing in the middle. The garden of Eden could not have been more delightful. Training the vines so high off the ground gives a great yield of grapes, which are not very highly flavoured, and which tend never quite fully to ripen. It is in this sense that the wines are green, coming from slightly under-ripe grapes. They are not at all green in colour. Much of their charm comes from their gentle pétillance, brought about by a fermentation that takes place after they are bottled. Light in alcohol, they are really delightful, drunk on a hot summer's day, though for export they tend, alas, to be sweetened and sometimes even have extra bubbles pumped in. Personally I prefer the white wines to the pink, and the pink to the red, which is strange, dark, astringent stuff.

Moving further inland, a certain amount of table wine, known as *consumo* is grown up the Douro valley, in the port wine district. Both red and white can be excellent, but they are only grown in limited quantities and are never likely to be exported. To the west of this area, however, lies the headquarters of one of the most popular of all Portuguese wines, Mateus Rosé. The demand is such now that not all of it can be grown in one place, but it originated in Quinta da Avelada, near Penafiel, at about the place where the vinho verde vineyards practically meet those of port. Much of the wine used today comes from higher in the Douro valley, and the bubbles are put in by the artifice of man rather than by nature, but the result has become uniquely popular.

The finest of all Portuguese wines are grown in the Dão area around Viseu. The vineyards are high up, as vineyards go – about two thousand feet – which provides a relatively cool mountain climate with lots of rain in winter and sunny, hot summers. It is this which gives the best of them (but by no means all) a degree of delicacy which one would hardly expect from a wine grown so far south. And some of the red wines are lightened by being vinified with a proportion of white grapes. The best of them age very well in bottle, and those that are now available in this country are remarkably good value. The cheapest are massive, hearty things – good quaffing wines without any of the delicacy that the more expensive wines of the area can achieve.

To the west of the Dão, good table wines, of all three colours, are grown around Bairrada and a certain amount of sparkling wine which, while quite unable to compete with champagne, has a strong and agreeable flavour of its own. Although sparkling wines are produced in other areas of Portugal, that of Bairrada is perhaps the best. Of the various vineyards around Lisbon, Colares is of special interest: it is one of the few remaining vineyards in Europe where there is no phylloxera, as the vines are planted in the sea sand where the louse cannot penetrate. The roots of the vine are in fact planted in the clay beneath the sand which has to be excavated to a great depth, involving considerable hazards for the workers. And the cost of planting is so high that it is questionable how long these wines will continue to be grown. A little undistinguished white wine is grown, but the best red Colares are comparable to Rhône wines and age well. The next area, Carcavellos, grow good white and red wines which were formerly imported into Britain under the name of

Lisbon. Here it is the white wines that are most worth looking for: they are fortified, so that they are fairly strong, and come in a wide range of sweetness. It is thanks to this that they tend to be likened to sherry, which is most unfair. They are things apart. Another nearby region, Bucellas, used to be popular in this country and its wine was often sold misleadingly as 'Portuguese hock'. It is one of the most agreeable of all Portuguese white wines, being fairly light, pleasantly acid, and having a good bouquet which increases with bottle age, but it is certainly not at all like hock; it has a distinctly more southern flavour and generally has a very earthy after-taste.

To the south of Lisbon lies Setúbal, best known for luscious, golden moscatels – admirable dessert wines. The best of these age well in bottle. For map see p. 129.

POSSET A posset could be taken by the most temperate at almost any time as it was supposed to prevent one from getting a cold if one had not got one, or to cure the cold if one had got one. The basic kind was made of hot milk, hot ale, sugar and nutmeg, but the wealthier hypochondriac could substitute sherry in place of beer.

POTCHEEN Illicitly stilled Irish whiskey.

POUILLY Two quite different French wines share this distinguished name: Pouilly-fuissé from Burgundy, and pouilly blanc fumé from the Loire valley. See BURGUNDY and LOIRE.

POURRITURE NOBLE See NOBLE ROT.

PREMIÈRES CÔTES DE BORDEAUX See BORDEAUX, WHITE AND CLARET.

PRESS A device used to crush the grapes so to extract the juice or must for fermentation. The pressing must be gentle so that the stalks and pips are not crushed, as otherwise unpleasant oils enter the wine that quite spoil the flavour, and once there they can never be got rid of. The simplest device is the human foot, and this method was used until recently in the port wine area where labour was cheap, but even there it is now proving uneconomic. As far back as the ancient Greek and Egyptian civilizations, mechanical presses of various kinds were invented and used. The Greeks invented the beam press, using the mechanical principle of a lever. A great beam of wood, twenty or thirty feet long, was pivoted at one end between a pair of upright pillars. A strong container for the fruit was put near the pillars, and the beam bore down on a wooden lid which did the crushing. This was later improved by the addition of a screw to work the beam. Such presses were still in regular use until the nineteenth century, and many examples are found in wine museums. The Greeks also invented a screw press in which the screw operated directly on the pressing platform. This became the principal form of press for use throughout the world, and so it remains to this day. The usual form is a straight sided barrel with small gaps between the staves, the lid being operated by the screw. During the nineteenth century, hydraulic presses were invented but these were originally too fierce, and the wines produced by them gave mechanical presses a bad name which they did not deserve. Hydraulic presses are now made to which this does certainly not apply. A modern variant on the screw press is made horizontally, with the screw being operated through an arrangement of gearing which results in a very gradual application of pressure. The ancient Egyptians used a totally different method: torsion. The juice was extracted by wringing the grapes in a bag made of cloth or matting. A variant on this was until very recently used in making sherry. One of the most modern presses is also a variation on this theme. This is the pneumatic press, perhaps best of all. It consists of a horizontal stainless steel cylinder in the centre of which is a strong rubber bag. The cylinder is filled with grapes and the bag is blown up by air pressure, squeezing the grapes against the side.

PRICKED See PIQUE.

PROOF SPIRIT Before the days of exact scientific measurement, it was necessary to determine some scale of spirit strength. Since this happened at so early a date, it is not surprising that the scale evolved was fundamentally absurd, like the Fahrenheit scale of temperature but, like the Fahrenheit scale, it worked and continues to work. The popular account given of its origin is that it is that strength of spirit which, when mixed with gunpowder, contains enough alcohol for the gunpowder still to ignite; be that as it may, it is now defined as 'that which at the temperature 51 degrees Fahrenheit weighs exactly 12/13ths of an equal measure of distilled water.' As this definition implies, it is measured in practice in terms of specific gravity by means of a hydrometer invented by one Sikes, a customs official. In the United States a somewhat different scale is used. To make matters more complicated, proof in this country is generally measured at 60 degrees Fahrenheit, at which temperature proof spirit contains 49.3 per cent by weight or 57.1 per cent by volume of alcohol. The table on the next page (reproduced by kind permission of 'Wine & Spirit Trade International') gives a comparison between the various scales.

PROVENCE See FRANCE, THE LESSER KNOWN WINES.

PULIGNY-MONTRACHET See BURGUNDY.

PUNCH Punch is one of those drinks with an antique ring about it – once very popular but now only too seldom found. It all began when the English took Jamaica from Spain in 1655 and were introduced to the drink made with rum, water and sugar, flavoured with fresh fruits. It could be served piping hot or ice cold, and soon became very popular. During the eighteenth century it became particularly popular with the whigs. It was mixed at table by the host in a great punch bowl, ladled out with a silver ladle, and served in silver cups, ornamental glasses, or rummers. Other spirits soon came to be added, particularly brandy. A recipe much favoured by the late Professor Saintsbury was as follows:

    3 parts of rum,
    2 of brandy,
    1 of lemon juice,
    6 of hot water, and
    sugar to taste.

There are as many recipes as there are punch fanciers, the only secret being that the mixture should be so contrived that nothing predominates, so that it tastes like a composition rather than a mixture. If lemons are used, the whole fruit should be put in, cutting the peel very thin to get the full flavour and scent from the cells near the surface, but the juice should be strained. Tea is often used in preference to water. Here are a few old recipes:

The Prince Regent's rum punch (1820)
Take 4 oz. of sugar, thin peel of 1 lemon and 1 Seville orange,

ALCOHOLIC STRENGTHS

British Isles (Sikes). Proof Spirit, per cent or degrees at 60°F.	France, Belgium (Gay-Lussac). Alcohol by Volume, per cent 59°F.	Austria, Italy, Russia (Tralles) Alcohol by Volume per cent 60°F.	U.S.A. Proof Spirit, per cent	Germany. Alcohol by Weight, per cent
2·5	1·4	1·4	2·8	1·1
5·0	2·8	2·9	5·7	2·3
7·5	4·2	4·3	8·5	3·4
10	5·6	5·7	11·4	4·6
12·5	7·0	7·1	14·3	5·7
15	8·5	8·6	17·2	6·9
17·5	9·9	10·0	20·0	8·0
20	11·3	11·4	22·8	9·2
22·5	12·7	12·8	25·7	10·4
25	14·2	14·3	28·6	11·6
27·5	15·6	15·7	31·5	12·8
30	17·1	17·2	34·4	14·0
32·5	18·5	18·6	37·3	15·1
35	19·9	20·1	40·2	16·4
37·5	21·3	21·5	43·0	17·5
40	22·7	22·9	45·8	18·7
42·5	24·1	24·2	48·6	19·8
45	25·5	25·6	51·5	21·0
47·5	26·9	27·1	54·4	22·2
50	28·4	28·6	57·3	23·5
52·5	29·8	30·0	60·1	24·7
55	31·3	31·5	63·0	25·9
57·5	32·7	32·9	65·9	27·1

British Isles (Sikes). Proof Spirit, per cent or degrees at 60°F.	France, Belgium (Gay-Lussac). Alcohol by Volume, per cent 59°F.	Austria, Italy, Russia (Tralles) Alcohol by Volume per cent 60°F.	U.S.A. Proof Spirit, per cent	Germany. Alcohol by Weight, per cent
60	34·2	34·4	68·8	28·4
62·5	35·6	35·8	71·7	29·6
65	37·1	37·3	74·6	30·9
67·5	38·5	38·7	77·4	32·1
70	39·9	40·1	80·2	33·4
72·5	41·3	41·5	83·0	34·6
75	42·7	42·9	85·8	35·9
77·5	44·1	44·3	88·6	37·2
80	45·6	45·8	91·4	38·5
82·5	47·0	47·1	94·2	39·8
85	48·4	48·5	97·0	41·1
87·5	49·8	49·9	99·9	42·4
90	51·2	51·4	o.p.2·8	43·8
92·5	52·6	52·8	5·6	45·1
95	54·0	54·2	8·5	46·5
97·5	55·4	55·6	11·3	47·9
100 or proof	56·9	57·1	14·2	49·3
o.p.2·5	58·3	58·5	17·1	50·7
5	59·8	60·0	20·0	52·1
7·5	61·2	61·4	22·8	53·5
10	62·7	62·9	25·7	55·0
12·5	64·1	64·3	28·5	56·4

British Isles (Sikes). Proof Spirit, per cent or degrees at 60°F.	France, Belgium (Gay-Lussac). Alcohol by Volume, per cent 59°F.	Austria, Italy, Russia (Tralles) Alcohol by Volume per cent 60°F.	U.S.A. Proof Spirit, per cent	Germany. Alcohol by Weight, per cent
15	65·6	65·7	31·3	57·9
17·5	67·0	67·1	34·1	59·4
20	68·5	68·6	37·0	60·9
22·5	69·9	70·0	39·9	62·3
25	71·3	71·4	42·8	63·9
27·5	72·7	72·8	45·6	65·4
30	74·1	74·2	48·4	67·0
32·5	75·5	75·6	51·3	68·6
35	77·0	77·1	54·2	70·2
37·5	78·4	78·5	57·0	71·8
40	79·8	79·9	59·9	73·4
42·5	81·2	81·4	62·7	75·0
45	82·7	82·8	65·6	76·7
47·5	84·1	84·2	68·4	78·4
50	85·5	85·6	71·3	80·1
52·5	86·9	87·0	74·2	81·9
55	88·4	88·5	77·1	83·7
57·5	89·8	89·9	79·9	84·3
60	91·2	91·3	82·7	87·2
62·5	92·6	92·7	85·5	89·5
65	94·1	94·2	88·3	91·1
67·5	95·5	95·7	91·3	93·2
70	97·0	97·2	94·3	95·3

114

1 bottle of dry champagne: ½ bottle of white brandy,
½ gill of rum, ½ gill of arrack,
½ gill of pineapple juice, 1 wine glass of Maraschino;
pour 1 quart of boiling water over 2 teaspoonfuls of green tea;
let it stand five minutes; strain, and mix with other ingredients;
pass through a sieve; let it remain in ice 30 minutes.

Bannister's Milk Punch (1829)
Pare 18 lemons very thin;
steep the same three days in 1 quart rum;
then add 2 quarts brandy;
the juice of 9 Seville oranges and 9 lemons,
3 quarts of water;
3 lb. of sugar;
and 2 grated nutmegs;
when the sugar is dissolved, mix thoroughly; add 2 quarts
scalded milk; cover, and let stand two hours; filter it and bottle;
when required for use, it should be iced 20 minutes before
drinking.

Gin Punch à la Burroughs
Juice of 1 lemon,
1 gill of pineapple juice,
1 pint of gin,
1 quart of tea (green).
If preferred as a cool punch, use broken ice instead of tea.

Whisky Punch
Juice and peel of 1 lemon in ½ pint of whisky, sweetened to
taste; water ad libitum.

PUTTONYOS See TOKAY.

QUARTS DE CHAUME See LOIRE.

RACKING The process of pouring the clear wine off the sediment
or lees in a cask which is done a number of times in the course of
maturation.

RAINWATER See MADEIRA.

RATAFIA A sweetened wine aperitif.

RAUENTHAL See RHINE.

RECTIFICATION See DISTILLATION AND RECTIFICATION.

RED, WHITE AND ROSÉ These are the three natural colours for wine to be. Most grapes, even black grapes, when they are pressed, have colourless juice which, if fermented, would result in a white wine. Red wines come about when the juice, or *must*, remains in contact with the grape skins long enough to pick up their colour. Thus, white champagne can be made from black grapes by separating the must from the skins very quickly. Most wines, however, are blanc-de-blancs, that is to say white wines made from white grapes, champagne being a rare exception. On the other hand, red wines must be made from black grapes, though a certain amount of must from white grapes is also used in some red wines. Pink, or *rosé* wines, are made either from black grapes, leaving the must in contact with the skins only for a short time, or from a mixture of grapes, or even (the poorer ones) made by blending red and white wines.

RETSINA See GREEK WINES.

RHEIN See RHINE.

RHEINGAU See RHINE.

RHEINHESSEN See RHINE.

RHEINPFALZ See RHINE.

RHENISH An old English term applied not only to Rhine wines but to all German wines.

RHINE, THE The Rhine comprises five quite separate areas: the Mittelrhein, the Rheingau, the Rheinhessen, the Nahe, and the Palatinate. Not surprisingly, a great variety of wine is grown, ranging from the driest to the very sweet indeed (see GERMAN WINE TERMS).

The Mittelrhein, or Middle Rhine, stretches all the way from Koblenz to the point where the River Nahe joins the Rhine. But although large, it is an area notable for its scenery rather than for the quality of its wines, which tend to be thin and acid save in the very best years. Much of it goes to make German sparkling wine (sekt).

The Rheingau, on the other hand, produces some of the very finest wines in Germany. It is on the right or northern bank of the river, facing almost due south, and has the Taunus mountains behind it to protect it from the cold north winds. The great

Riesling vine is grown there predominantly, providing wines that are rich in flavour, with plenty of sugar and ample alcohol. Yet, although these wines are big by any standards, they have quite exceptional elegance and finesse. The area stretches between Assmannshausen and Hochheim. The former town, although geographically within the area, hardly seems to be within it spiritually, and specializes in producing red wines grown from the Pinot Noir vine, known locally as the Spätburgunder. They are rather surprising in character, giving the impression of being white wines disguised as reds. But after Assmannshausen come a succession of great names: Rüdesheim, Geisenheim, Winkel (in the hills behind which are two of the finest estates in the Rheingau, Schloss Vollrads and Schloss Johannisberg), Johannisberg, Mittelheim, Oestrich, Hallgarten, Hattenheim, Steinberg, Marcobrunnen, Kiedrich, Rauenthal, Martinsthal, Eltville, and finally Hochheim. These wines tend to need a certain amount of time to mature, though it is hard to be specific as it depends on the year for the quality. Most need at least five years and some as many as ten. They remain good for twice as long or sometimes longer.

The Rheinhessen lies on the left bank of the river, not quite opposite the Rheingau, the finest sites being upstream, between Worms and Mainz. It stretches quite a long way inland, though most of the finest wines are grown near the river. They are slighter, less subtle, and quicker to mature than those of the Rheingau, nor do they last so long in bottle, often being past their best when less than eight years old. Apart from the wines grown in individual vineyards, the area is noted for its liebfraumilch (see GERMAN WINE TERMS). Travelling again from north to south, the most noteworthy towns are Bingen, Mainz, Nackenheim, Neirstein (whose finest wines are second only to the great growths of the Rheingau, though one should utter a word of warning: Niersteiner Domtal does not necessarily come from Neirstein at all but is a generic name), Oppenheim, and Worms.

The Nahe is a law unto itself. Lying between the Rhine and the Moselle, its wines tend to combine some of the most attractive features of each, and it is the subject of a separate article.

The Palatinate (in Germany, the Pfalz or Rheinpfalz), is an exception amongst the great wine districts of Germany in that its vineyards do not lie along the banks of a river. There are three separate areas: the Unterhaardt, or Lower Palatinate; the Mittel-haardt, or Middle Palatinate; and the Oberhaardt, or Upper Palatinate. Leading towards Alsace, its climate is amongst the most pleasant in Germany, with lots of sunshine and limited rainfall; and it is this which gives the wines much of their character. Although they tend somewhat to be lacking in delicacy and finesse, they make up for it with their full flavoured mellow-ness. The Riesling, however, produces very fine wines, particularly in the Middle Palatinate. It is the sweeter wines which are generally the most attractive, as the sweetness balances the strong flavour. A certain number of Gewürtztraminer grapes are grown, giving a foretaste of Alsace. The most distinguished sites are in the Middle Palatinate at Kallstadt, Ungstein, Bad Dürkheim, Wachenheim, Forst, Deidesheim and Ruppertsberg. The very best areas are Wachenheim, Forst and Deidesheim. Like the wines of the Rheinhessen, those of the Palatinate can attain maturity at quite an early age, but the best of them last longer.

All Rhine wines are bottled in tall brown bottles. Like all white wines, Rhine wines should be served slightly chilled. They are incredibly versatile and go well with almost any kind of food, choosing a wine of the right degree of sweetness as a matter of common sense. They are particularly good with all sorts of fish, poultry, and white meat like veal. The very finest, very sweet wines taste at their best without any food at all, taken by them-selves, preferably after the meal.

RHONE The wines grown along the banks of the River Rhône – red, white and rosé – although less widely esteemed than those of Bordeaux and Burgundy, are undoubtedly amongst the finest wines grown in France or the world. The best wines are grown in two distinct and relatively compact areas. The more northerly of these is elongated, stretching roughly between Vienne and Valence. The other is further south, more or less square in shape, and centred around Orange. It is not surprising that in so large an area many good wines are grown, varying considerably in styles. The remarkable thing is that they all have a substantial family resemblance. They are robust, well flavoured, and tend to be very long-lived. And because of the southerly latitude, the vintage tends to be more consistent than in Burgundy, with fewer failures. The broad classification of these wines is côtes du rhône, which includes all the good but not especially distinguished wines that are grown around the more limited areas providing fine wines. A somewhat more limited appellation is côtes-du-rhône villages.

The most northerly of the great Rhône wines, and perhaps the best red of them all, is côte-rôtie, grown on almost precipitous hillsides just south of Vienne. Although it is divided into five specific areas, these fall in two parts: the Côte-Blonde and the Côte-Brune. Most of the wine is red, and the best balance is achieved by blending from the two areas. They generally need to be kept for at least twelve years before they are really ready, and live without fading for thirty or forty years in bottle.

Just south of the Côte-Rôtie comes Condrieu, which provides some of the best dry wines in the valley. Within the area is the remarkable, though minute vineyard of Château-Grillet – the smallest to have an appellation contrôlée of its own – producing a minute output of world famous dry white wine. Even the lighter vintages require six or seven years in bottle before they show their best, and the better years need much longer. Further to the south and on the east side of the river, another of the great wines is grown: hermitage. Most of the wine is red, though the production of white wine is not insignificant. The red wines are vast in flavour, forceful in character, and have a purple red colour that is all their own. They are amongst the most long-lived of all, and should normally be kept for ten years before being drunk. When too young, they are too rough and coarse to be enjoyable. They rarely show their best until twenty years old, and seem to last for ever. White hermitage is amber coloured, dry, but mellow in flavour. These wines also take at least ten years to mature, and live in bottle for a very long time. Apart from hermitage proper, vineyards in the same general area produce the lesser wine croizes-hermitage. The best white wine from hereabouts, grown near the village of Mercurol, is chante-alouette.

On the opposite side of the river is Saint-Joseph, providing distinguished red and white wines, while further to the south, also on the western bank of the river, are the vineyards of Cornas also giving good red wines. Further still to the south, are the vineyards of Saint-Péray, growing white wines which are often made sparkling, tend to be rather sweet, and are not at all distinguished.

The most famous wine from the area around Orange is châteauneuf-du-pape. While both red and white wines are grown there, the former are more famous and, rather surprisingly, are distinctly lighter than those grown further north, maturing much more quickly, and being very agreeable when only three year's old, though they tend to be better still after six or seven years.

An unusual wine grown nearby is muscat de beaumes-de-venise – a sweet, slightly fortified wine that tends to be heavy, heady and sticky; but the best examples can be very good indeed.

In the south-west of this area, a sun-scorched plateau surrounded by hills provides some of the finest rosé wine grown anywhere: tavel rosé. It is one of the few rosés that keep well, and is usually only at its best after four or five years in bottle. The neighbouring commune of Lirac produces softer, aromatic rosé wines which mature more quickly, and a certain amount of delicious, robust red wine is also grown there.

RICHEBOURG   See BURGUNDY.

RIOJA   See SPANISH TABLE WINES.

ROMANÉE-CONTI   One of the most famous of the red wine vineyards in Burgundy. It is only about four and a half acres in extent, and the demand is such that the prices are astronomical. Excellent though the wines undoubtedly are, the quality scarcely justifies the price that they now fetch. Until 1945 it was planted entirely with native vines which involved enormous expense to keep down the phylloxera. During the war, the work involved became impossible, and the vineyard had to be replanted so that the immediate post-war vintages are amongst the poorest that it has ever produced. Young vines never produce such good wines as old ones, and the deterioration of quality which has taken place since may well be attributed to the relative youth of the vines rather than to the fact that they are now grafted, though grafting may also have had quite a lot to do with it. The same company owns the famous La Tâche vineyard, and part of Le Richebourg, etc. These other wines are estate bottled with appropriate variants of the famous Romanée-Conti label.

ROMANIA   The vineyards of Romania are old established, and

wines of good quality are grown there in a variety of styles, though the export trade has only recently built up to any substantial size. One of the best of the wines that is generally available is a sweetish wine sold under the varietal name of muscat ottonel.

ROTA TENT A very dark red wine formerly made by a special process of vinification at Rota in the south of Spain, on the edge of the sherry area. The vineyards have now been absorbed by an American naval base.

ROUSSETTE See FRANCE, THE LESSER KNOWN WINES.

ROUSSILLON See FRANCE, THE LESSER KNOWN WINES.

RÜDESHEIM See RHINE.

RUM Rum is a spirit distilled from fermented molasses or (more rarely) sugar cane syrup, both of which ferment very quickly and easily. Like whisky, rum can be distilled either in continuous (patent) stills or in pot stills, and the choice has a similar sort of effect on the product: the former rums are lighter in style, the latter heavier and more powerfully flavoured. Rum can be made wherever there is sugar cane but is mostly produced in the West Indies, notably Barbados, Jamaica, Guyana, Trinidad, Cuba, Puerto Rico, Martinique, Santo Domingo, and Haiti. Each has its own variety of styles. When distilled, it is generally colourless, or almost so. The colour of the old, traditional brown rums (the sort of rum that Chesterton was thinking of when he wrote 'You will find me drinking rum, like a sailor in a slum...') was derived either from ageing in oak casks or from molasses or both. Rum can, however, be matured without imparting much colour at all, for instance in old casks from which the tannin has already been abstracted. It is these light rums (particularly associated in the past with Cuba, but now produced in Jamaica and elsewhere) that are gaining rapidly in popularity, especially drunk as daiquiri cocktail (see COCKTAIL) but also often drunk with fruit juices, water, soda water, or Coca Cola. A word of warning here: it is sometimes supposed that these colourless spirits are weaker or less potent than the darker ones. They are not. The traditional dark rums from Jamaica, Martinique and Trinidad are taken neat, with water (as grog – the traditional navy drink), with aniseed, or in the form of a punch (see COLLINS, PUNCH).

RUMMER   An eighteenth century English glass with a large bowl on a short stem. Its main purpose was for drinking punch.

RUSSIA   As becomes the leading Communist country, the emphasis appears to be on growing wines for the masses rather than fine wines, and the Russians have a taste for very sweet sparkling wines which is shared by few. The best of the wines are grown in Armenia, Georgia, The Caucasus, The Crimea, and Moldavia, but those so far exported show no distinction.

RUWER   See MOSELLE.

RYE   See WHISKY.

SAAR   See MOSELLE.

SACK   Although there has been considerable and heated dispute as to the origin of the word 'sack', it is now generally accepted that it comes from the Spanish verb *sacar*, meaning to draw out; sacks, therefore, were wines exported from Spanish speaking countries. The most famous of all, of course, was sherry sack, praised by Shakespeare through the mouth of Falstaff, but Canary sack was also popular as was Malligo sack, from Malaga, later called Mountain. Thanks to the popularity of these sack wines, however, the term came into wider use and Pepys's *Diary*, for instance, contains a reference to raspberry sack, which is believed to be a kind of mead.

SAINT-AMOUR   See BURGUNDY.

SAINE-CROIX-DU-MOT   See BORDEAUX, WHITE.

SAINT EMILION   See CLARET.

SAINT ESTÈPHE   See CLARET.

SAINT JOSEPH   See RHÔNE.

SAINT JULIEN   See CLARET.

SAINT NICHOLAS DE BOURGUEIL   See LOIRE.

SAINT PÉRAY   See RHÔNE.

SAINT RAPHAEL   See APERITIF.

SAKE   A colourless Japanese beverage made from fermenting rice, and sometimes (though wrongly) referred to as rice wine. It is quite high in alcohol, about equal to a normal sherry, and is drunk with various ceremonial rituals in its country of origin. It has a pleasant and unique taste and goes well with Japanese food.

SAMOS   See GREEK WINES.

SANCERRE   See LOIRE.

SANGIOVESE   See ITALIAN WINES.

SANGRIA   Is the famous red wine cup of Spain, and there are as many recipes as there are Spanish restaurants. The basis is a lot of fruit – commonly oranges, lemons and peaches – with a bottle of Spanish red wine and about half a bottle of soda water. Sometimes sugar is added and, in Spain, brandy is commonly added too, but elsewhere the cost of brandy is prohibitive, and anyhow the idea is to please rather than to intoxicate. It should be well iced, and makes an admirable summer drink.

SANTENAY   See BURGUNDY.

SARDINIA   See ITALIAN WINES.

SASSELLA   See ITALIAN WINES.

SAUMUR   See LOIRE.

SAUTERNES   See BORDEAUX, WHITE.

SAVIGNY   See BURGUNDY.

SAVOY   See FRANCE, THE LESSER KNOWN WINES.

SCHLOSSBÖCKELHEIM   See NAHE.

SCHLOSS JOHANNISBERG   See RHINE.

SCHLOSS VOLLRADS   See RHINE.

SCHNAPPS   See AQUAVIT.

SCHOPPENWEIN   German vin ordinaire.

SEC   French for 'dry'. Like the English word, it generally means rather sweet.

SEDIMENT Sediment can occur in almost any wine, and should always occur in a naturally prepared red wine which is allowed to mature in bottle. If it does not, then it has artificially been removed, and the wine has lost something. It also occurs in white wines, largely in the form of small tartrate crystals. Owing to the public resistance to this extremely natural by-product of maturation, an immense amount of trouble is taken by wine growers producing sherry, for example, and wood port, to eliminate all traces of sediment by such processes as ultra-cooling, in which the wine is reduced to a low temperature before bottling, so that any sediment that is likely to come out is removed. Many a good wine, however, has been damaged by taking too much out of it, and it is a pity that the public has not been educated to expect sediment and to decant their wines. Very little is lost by this process, and the wine can give of its best.

SEKT. German sparkling wine.

SERCIAL See MADEIRA.

SERVING WINE Serving wine is quite simple and calls for much less fuss than is usually made. If the wine has a sediment it should be decanted, but this does not apply to any normal white wine. Its temperature should be right, and since the appeal of a wine owes something to its colour and a lot to its aroma, it should be served in a plain, clear glass, leaving enough air space above the wine for the aroma to develop. Certain special glasses are referred to in the articles on certain of the wines, but if in doubt, use a good tulip shaped glass of ample size. See also CRADLES, DECANTERS, FOOD, WINE WITH, GLASSES, ICE and TEMPERATURE.

SETÚBAL See PORTUGUESE WINES.

SEYSSEL See FRANCE, THE LESSER KNOWN WINES.

SHANDY A mixture of beer with ginger beer or lemonade.

SHERRY Real sherry comes from Spain, but it has been flattered by having many imitators, some of which are very good wines. These have to be sold with additional geographical names, the best known being 'South African Sherry', 'Australian Sherry', 'Cyprus Sherry', and 'Californian Sherry'. Of these, the South

African wines tend to be the closest imitations and are very well made. It is a pity that they describe themselves as 'Sherry'.

Sherry is grown in Andalusia, around the old town of Jerez de la Frontera, known to the Arabs as *sherris,* from which the English word and the modern Spanish word are both derived. There are two basic kinds: fino and oloroso. A third kind – palo cortado – also exists but is seldom exported from Spain. All these come from the same grapes grown in the same vineyards, and which the must turns out to be when it is matured is largely a matter of chance. Must turning into fino develops a *flop* – a layer of yeast cells that grows on its surface and which profoundly affects its style. Fino sherry is light in colour and body, with a unique very penetrating aroma. Manzanilla is a special kind of fino, matured in the sea air at Sanlucar de Barrameda on the mouth of the Guadalquivir. It is very dry and fresh with a salt tang to it. Oloroso is darker and somewhat heavier, and although its name means 'fragrant', its aroma is deep and mellow, less assertive than a fino. Both kinds are bone dry. To make a sweet sherry, specially prepared sweetening wines have to be added. All sherry is matured by means of the solera system (which *see*).

As fino ages, its character changes subtly; it grows darker in colour and acquires a flavour and aroma that is generally described as 'nutty'. In fact it comes rather to resemble the wines of Montilla (which *see*) hence its name: amontillado. The term is widely misused simply to mean a medium dry sherry. A real amontillado is an old wine, and necessarily expensive, but worth it. A palo cortado has a bouquet very like that of an amontillado but a flavour more like a light oloroso. An amoroso is a lightish style of oloroso with a fair degree of sweetness. Cream sherries are lighter and sweeter still. Brown sherries are dark, heavy olorosos, made very sweet.

Fino sherry is best served chilled at about 50°F. Amontillados and medium sherries generally taste best very slightly chilled. Olorosos are normally best at room temperature. And as part of the joy of sherry lies in its superb fragrance, *all* sherries should be served in large glasses; copitas are best, but tulip shaped wine glasses are also very good. Neither should be more than one-third full. The worst glasses are pub glasses that go in at the middle and are filled to the top. They are inexcusable.

In contact with air, sherry oxidizes. This can be detected in dry sherries after two or three days, though kept at a steady 50° in a refrigerator, they last twice as long. Medium sherries last longer, and sweet sherries for as many weeks. It can be avoided either by buying the wine in half bottles or decanting half of a bottle into a half bottle and corking it tightly when it will last as if it had never been opened. Fino sherry deteriorates slowly in bottle, and should be drunk as quickly as possible. Medium sherries last longer and sweet sherries actually improve, their sweetness gradually being eaten away while they take on a special character of aroma described as 'bottle age'. To make this worth while, they have to be kept for at least ten years. Although so often drunk alone, sherries always taste much better if taken with a snack, known in Spanish as a *tapa*.

SICILY   See ITALIAN WINES.

SLING   See CUP.

SMOKING   It has often been suggested that smoking spoils the palate for wine, but this is totally disproved by the fact that many of the most renowned wine tasters are also heavy smokers. It is perhaps true to say, though, that the best wine tasters are seldom heavy *cigarette* smokers. While smoking at the right time does not seem to have much effect upon the palate, however, it is certainly fatal to the enjoyment of wine to smoke while drinking it. The one exception to this appears to be sherry, and that is certainly not enhanced by smoking. It makes very little difference to the enjoyment of spirits, or long drinks such as beer.

SOAVE   See ITALIAN WINES.

SODA WATER   is made by pumping carbon dioxide into water. When first produced in the eighteenth century it was believed to be good for health, and bicarbonate of soda was sometimes added, hence its name. Other salts were occasionally added to give, for instance, potash water. The soda water siphon, which is popular in Britain but seldom found in the United States, dates from the first quarter of the nineteenth century. Many old ones are still to be found which produced soda water from Seidlitz powders. These were sold in two separate packages, one containing tartaric acid and salts thereof, while the other contained sodium bicarbonate. One half was dissolved in water and the other put dry into a second compartment of the siphon. When the siphon was inverted, the two parts came together and the carbon dioxide was evolved. The seidlitz-powder is immortalized in the well-known epitaph.

Here lies the body of Margaret Crowther,
Who died through drinking a seidlitz-powder.
Oh! may her soul in Heaven be blessed:
But she should have waited till it effervessed.

SOLERA The solera system is a continuous method of maturattion which consists of fractional blending. It has not been found successful for all wines, but is extremely successful for the maturation of sherry and madeira. It is also widely used in Spain for making Spanish brandies. The system is this. If a shipper has a cask of a wine that he likes and he takes away a small part of it (perhaps a third), filling in the void with a similar wine but younger, then after a while the young wine takes on all the quality of the old and he is back where he started. He can do this indefinitely and over a great many stages, or *scales*, so that he finishes up with a solera system, containing perhaps a dozen scales (each consisting of a number of casks containing practically identical wine) the youngest scale being fed with freshly fermented wine, and the oldest giving the mature wine that he needs. After a while the solera settles down completely into a state of equilibrium so that the quality of the wine never varies provided that it is operated continuously in the same way.

SOMMELIER Wine waiter.

SOUTH AFRICA Wine was first produced in South Africa in 1659. During the eighteenth and first half of the nineteenth century, the sweet wines from Constantia were regarded amongst the finest in the world. Unhappily towards the end of the nineteenth century they suffered a total eclipse, brought about partly by over-production, which drastically lowered their quality, and partly by Gladstone's policy of reducing the tax on French wines in 1861, which deprived them of their preferential tariff. With the phylloxera following in 1885, South African wines virtually disappeared from the world market. In 1918 the Co-operative Wine Growers Association of South Africa Limited (better known as the K.W.V.) was founded to reorganize the trade, and within ten years exports were resumed, the English side of the trade being

handled since 1931 by the the South African Wine Farmers'
Association (London) Limited which is controlled by the K.W.V.
There are two viticultural areas, the coastal belt stretching
inland north-east from Cape Town as far as Tulbagh and Ceres;
and the Little Karoo stretching roughly from Worcester in the
west to Oudtshoorn in the east. The coastal belt includes Stellenbosch, Paarl, Tulbagh and Constantia – the districts in which most
of the finest wines are grown. Excellent dry white and red wines
are grown there together with a substantial proportion of wines
vinified to imitate sherry and port. These latter are very good
wines in their own right, and it is a pity that they tend to lose
out by comparison with the wines they imitate. Taken on their
own merits, and offered as an alternative to the wines of Spain
and Portugal, rather than as imitations, they could well compete.
Little Karoo also produces South African sherries together with
with sweet wines and brandies. White and red table wines of excellent quality have been produced for many years now, the Stein
grape giving a white wine of marked individuality. The South
African wine growers face difficulties of nomenclature stemming
from their original policy of imitating the wines of other districts.
It is to be hoped that these will be overcome and their wines
recognized to be excellent products they undoubtedly are.

SOUTH AMERICA   See page 15.

SPANISH TABLE WINES   Spain is one of the best countries for a
wine drinker to travel around, as it enjoys a great variety of
climates, from the cool north-western area, dominated by the
Atlantic, to the sun-baked vineyards of Andalusia in the south-
east. Although it is fair to say that no truly great table wine is
grown there, nearly all the wines are well made and the variety
is enormous.

SPAIN AND PORTUGAL

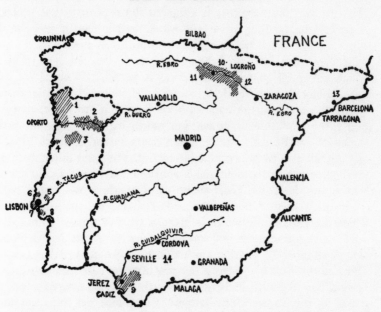

1 Vinho Verde. 2 Port. 3 Dao. 4 Agueda, Barraida. 5 Bucelas. 6 Colares.
7 Carcavelos. 8 Setubal. 9 Sherry. 10 Rioja Alavesa. 11 Rioja Alta. 12
   Rioja Baja. 13 Alella. 14 Montilla-Moriles.

The cool north-west grows very light wines, mostly white,
many of them resembling those delicious and much better known
freaks, the *vinhos verdes* of Portugal. Travelling eastwards, just
south of the Pyrenees lies the area of Rioja, where the finest red
and white table wines are grown. This is itself divided into three
parts: Alta, Alavesa and Baja. The finest wines are grown in the

first two, the best of which have considerable finesse. Those of the Rioja Baja, on the other hand, are strong and unsubtle. Most wines sold commercially are blended from several vineyards and years so that they bear only vague indications of age, such as 4° año – a wine four years old. The best, however, are genuine vintage wines and are so marked. Red wines vary from the austere and delicate kinds that are likely to appeal to claret lovers, through a range of bigger bodied wines that are closer to the style of burgundy, and finally wines of gross size and little breeding. Likewise with white wines, some are dry, fresh and delicate, while others are sweet and heavy. The best buys are usually the cheapest and most expensive, either of the reds or of the whites. Some of the medium price red wines (and a few of the cheap ones) are too sweet, which makes them positively nasty.

Moving eastwards into Aragon, the area to look for is Cariñena, which grows all colours of wine but is particularly noted for its light coloured and delicious *rosados*. Moving yet further eastwards to the coast, the best wines of Catalonia are white, particularly those of Alella, grown just north of Barcelona, on two slopes of granite soil, one of which has a rather northern aspect and produces light wines of high acidity, while the other, with a great exposure to the sun, yields wines of the opposite character. Further to the north, the Castillo de Perelada grows sound red, white and *rosado* table wines and also a light sparkling wine which leapt into fame when its growers were restrained from calling it *champagne* in the law suit of *Bollinger* v. *Costa Brava Wine Co.* A number of sparkling wines are grown in Catalonia and some of the best come from the southern part of that province, around San Sadurni de Noya. The red, white and *rosado* wines grown in the Panadés area around Villafranca del Panadés can also be excellent, as can the Majorcan red wines grown around Benisalem, which are quite unexpectedly delicate and delicious, the best vintage wines attaining, with age, a considerable degree of finesse.

The most famous area in the southern half of Spain is Valdepeñas, producing big, earthy wines of all colours. On the coast, Tarragona is best known for its sweet red wine which resembles port, but none of its wines is of any quality. Better wines are grown further south near Valencia and Alicante, the most famous historically being Benicarlo, which used to be used in Bordeaux for blending, to add colour and strength to the clarets. Some are so dark as to be almost black. Much further to the south, beyond the sherry country (where the weather is cooler, thanks again to the Atlantic influence) excellent white wines are grown around Huelva, under the name *vinos del Condado da Niebla.*

SPARKLING WINES The sparkle comes from carbon dioxide – the same gas which gives the bubbles in soda water. As it is one of the natural products of fermentation, it is easy to make a wine that sparkles simply by bottling it before the fermentation is complete. But to make a really good sparkling wine is one of the most difficult and expensive things that a wine grower can undertake. The classic way of doing it is by the *méthode champenoise* which, as its name indicates, originated in Champagne and which is the only method used for making that wine. By this method, after an appropriate blend has been made of fully fermented wines, a second fermentation in bottle is provoked by adding a small amount of syrup together with an appropriate yeast. At a cellar temperature of 50°F., four grams of sugar fermented in the bottle give a gas pressure of one atmosphere, though usually a pressure of five to six atmospheres is required. After the fermentation in bottle has been completed, the deposit which forms as a result of the fermentation is removed, generally by freezing the neck of the bottle in a freezing mixture so that the deposit can be removed (after it has been shaken down to the neck) in the middle of a little cylinder of ice, the void being made up by an addition of wine generally together with a *dosage* of sugar, so that the finished wine has the right degree of sweetness.

A cheaper way of making sparkling wine is by the method of *cuves-closes*, otherwise known as the Charmat, or tank method. Here the second fermentation is effected in a large container, so that the deposit formed can easily be filtered out. The method is not therefore so very different but carried out on a larger scale, which results in a somewhat different flavour, though the wines made by this method are very good. A cheaper method used, for instance, in making the Luxembourg *perlweine*, is to ferment the wine in tanks until most but not all the sugar has been used up, then to lower the temperature drastically so that the fermentation is slowed down, when the carbon dioxide produced is absorbed by the wine. It is then filtered under pressure and bottled.

The simplest and worst way is to take a cheap white wine and aerate it with carbon dioxide. This gives an inferior wine which rapidly loses its sparkle in the glass.

Sparkling wines are made all over the world, and vary in quality from the sublime wines of Champagne to perfectly appalling examples which are found in various places. Champagne, however, has by no means the monopoly of good sparkling wines, and excellent examples are to be found in most of the major wine growing countries.

SPRITZIG Much sought after characteristic found in German wines, particularly moselle, and caused by slight traces of carbon dioxide produced in the course of a malo-lactic fermentation in bottle. Found in young wines, it is no more than a sensation on the tongue, and falls far short of pétillance.

STARBOARD LIGHT Crème de Menthe.

STEINBERG See RHINE and KLOSTER EBERBACH.

STEINWEIN See FRANCONIA.

STELLENBOSCH See SOUTH AFRICA.

STILL See DISTILLATION AND RECTIFICATION.

STILL WINE A wine that does not sparkle.

STOUT See BEER.

STRAIGHT This term really has two meanings. Applied to a spirit as sold, it means one that is a product of a single distillation and not blended with a spirit of another kind. Applied to a drink as served, it means a spirit that has not been diluted with anything else.

STRAW See PAILLE.

STREGA See LIQUEUR.

STRENGTH See PROOF SPIRIT.

SUCRAGE See CHAPTALIZATION.

SULPHUR Sulphur has been used for many centuries in various ways to preserve wine, and to control the fermentation. It is also used in the vineyards as a remedy against fungus diseases. There is no harm in it provided that the right amount is used, but in cheap white wine often far too much is used to prevent the wine suffering a second fermentation, particularly when shipped in cask. Such wines are sometimes little better than infernal.

SWEETS A strange term found in England and meaning a liquor made of fruit and sugar with or without anything that has been fermented. It includes British wines mead and metheglin. The term is of little practical use today, but was widely used several centuries ago particularly in connection with fortified wines.

SWICKER A cheap blended white wine made from various grape varieties in Alsace.

SWITZERLAND Wine is grown in many parts of Switzerland, and many of them are delightful drunk locally, but the high elevation and mountain climate is hardly an ideal one for viticulture, and none of the wines is really notable; indeed some are so light as to put one in mind of water. The most important wine growing areas are the cantons of Valais, Neuchatel and Vaud, the two best known being the white fendant, and the red dole, both from Valais. Neuchatel is principally noted for its white wines, some of which are pétillant. A good red wine, always in short supply, is balgacher scholssberg, grown on the banks of the Rhine in the north-east mountains, where a white wine is also grown; both can be slightly pétillant. The Italian speaking canton of Ticino grows a red wine with a good reputation: merlot del Ticino.

SWIZZLE STICK An obscene invention used for removing the bubbles from champagne by swizzling it round. Anyone wishing to drink a still wine should buy a still wine instead of wasting a sparkling one.

TABLE WINES Any wine intended to be drunk at table with food, i.e. not a fortified wine.

TANNIN This is an important element in the flavour of wine, especially red wines. Astringent to the mouth, it is derived largely from the skin of the grapes. Without a sufficiency of tannin, no red wine will develop properly, and it is one of the things to look for in judging any young wine that it is intended to lay down. On the other hand, if there is too much tannin, it can overwhelm the other qualities of the wine, and while the wine seems to last for ever, it never becomes really enjoyable. The 1937 clarets are an example of this.

TAPA Small snack provided in Spain to enhance the pleasure of a glass of sherry.

TARRAGONA See SPANISH TABLE WINES.

TASTEVIN A shallow silver cup, more like a saucer to look at, with a handle to hold it by, and patterned indentations to reflect the colour of the wine. It is used for wine tasting in France, especially in Burgundy.

TASTING The technique of tasting is one that can only be acquired with experience, preferably helped by the assistance of the trade. In tasting wines, much is to be learnt by comparing successive vintages of the same wine, or wines of the same vintage but from different districts. Only experience, however, coupled with a good memory for flavours and aromas, will impart the skill to know how a wine is going to develop. It is foolish to taste too many wines at once. Half a dozen is a fair figure to begin with, and it is rarely possible even for an expert to taste more than about fifteen in one session. Good glasses should be used, the air should be clean, without the slightest trace of tobacco smoke, and it is a good idea to have a white table cloth to help in checking the colour. If red and white wines are tasted together, opinions differ as to which should be tasted first, but it is suggested that red is the preference. At a serious tasting the wine is not drunk. First the colour is examined, then it is sniffed, then it is rinsed round the mouth and spat out. Some tasters do, however, let the tiniest drops trickle down to complete the sensation and experts have developed a technique of drawing in a little air over the wine, further to activate the nose and palate; it is most effective but sounds revolting.

TAVEL See RHÔNE.

TEMPERANCE Temperance means moderation. All real wine lovers are temperate. A teetotaller is as intemperate as a drunk.

TEMPERATURE The temperature at which wine should be served has always been controversial, and the one thing to remember is that there is no absolute rule. Generally speaking, white wines (especially if they are sweet) taste best when they are served chilled, but not frozen stiff; about 50°F. is ideal. But there are exceptions such as tokay, which taste best at room temperature, as do some muscatels. Red wines are generally best served *chambré* – which means at room temperature, definitely not warmed and most definitely not perceptibly heated. This applies especially to claret, and many claret lovers find it best to let their wines acquire the temperature of the kitchen, by leaving them in that room for twenty-four hours before drinking, rather than the dining-room, especially if the latter is heated only just before the meal. On the other hand, many lovers of burgundy find that they taste best when very slightly cool, for instance at a cellar temperature of about 55°F. It is entirely a matter of personal preference. There has recently been a fashion for chilling young beaujolais as if it were a white wine, and there is no denying the fact that, served in this way, it makes an admirable aperitif. Should a wine be wanted in a hurry, never heat it too quickly by standing it next to the hot tank or mull it in front of a fire. Such treatment will spoil any wine. It is better to drink it cold or to raise the temperature with a hand round the glass. Putting the bottle in luke warm water (not hot) for a quarter of an hour does little harm though, or it can be decanted into a slightly warm decanter.

Temperature plays a very important part in the maturation of wines and spirits. With wines, the higher the temperature of the cellar or storage space, the quicker they mature and vice versa. It is also generally found that wines achieve their greatest potential when matured in relatively cool cellars, 50–55°F. being regarded as ideal. The main thing, though, is to keep the temperature even. Frequent changes of temperature, particularly if they are rapid, bring about an irreversible change in the wine which spoils it. Similar irreversible changes are brought about by very low or very high temperatures, so that it is most inadvisable to store wine for more than a short time in a refrigerator; on the other hand, the effect of high temperature is made good use of in the preparation of madeira (which see). Temperature also plays an important part in the maturation of spirits. Both whisky and brandy are matured above ground in wooden casks, and the effect of the warm summer air, with the contrasting cold winter air, is regarded as so important that some Scotch warehouses are heated in summer, but this is never necessary in Cognac owing to the warmer summers there.

TENT   See ROTA TENT.

TEQUILA   A strong, colourless distilled liquor prepared in Mexico from the fermented juice of the Century plant.

TERROIR   This means earth. The Goût de Terroir is an earthy taste apparent in wines grown on soil that is too heavy. It is particularly noticeable in the after-taste, and is generally regarded as very undesirable.

TIA MARIA   See LIQUEUR.

TIGERMILK   See YUGOSLAVIA.

TINTILLA   ROTA TENT.

TODDY   Toddy has a variety of meanings. To those of us in temperate climates it means a mixed drink flavoured with spirits and usually hot, though sometimes cold, especially in the U.S.A. To those who live in the tropics, it is a strong drink made by fermenting the juice of palm trees. The traditional toddy is made from equal quantities of spirits and hot water, sometimes with a squeeze of lemon peel, or some lemon juice, or herbs added. This is an old recipe for an apple toddy: put a baked apple in a glass; add 1 oz. of powdered sugar, 1 gill of brandy, ½ pint boiling cider; grate a little ginger on top and add a piece of lemon peel.

TOKAY   See HUNGARY.

TORBATO DI ALGHERO   See ITALIAN WINES.

TOURAINE   See LOIRE.

TRITTENHEIM   See MOSELLE.

TULBAGH   See SOUTH AFRICA.

TUNISIA   See AFRICA.

ULLAGE   The space between the surface of the wine and the cork or the top of a cask. If a faulty cork causes ullage in a bottle, it is more than probable that the wine will have gone bad.

ULTRA-COOLING   See SEDIMENT.

UNITED STATES OF AMERICA   See AMERICAN WINES.

VALAIS   See SWITZERLAND.

VALDEPEÑAS   See SPANISH TABLE WINES.

VALENCIA   See SPANISH TABLE WINES.

VALPATENA   See ITALIAN WINES.

VALPOLICELLA   See ITALIAN WINES.

VAN DER HUM   See LIQUEUR.

VARIETAL WINE   A wine named after the variety of grape from which it is vinified.

VAUD   See SWITZERLAND.

V.D.Q.S.   See APELLATION CONTRÔLÉE.

VERDELHO   See MADEIRA.

VERDICCHIO DEI CASTELLI DI JESI   See ITALIAN WINES.

VERMOUTH   White wine flavoured with various herbs and produced principally in France and Italy, French vermouths tending to be lighter and drier than the Italian ones.

VERNACCIA   See ITALIAN WINES.

VERNACCIA DI SAN GIMIGNANO   See ITALIAN WINES.

VIEILLE CURE   See LIQUEUR.

VIN DE L'ANNEE   Literally 'wine of the year'. A wine bottled soon after the vintage and intended for immediate drinking.

VINEGAR   The flavour of vinegar is provided by acetic acid, and acetic acid is produced (at any rate in true vinegars) by the action of *mycoderma aceti* on alcohol. The origin of the alcohol determines the style of the vinegar. Thus, malt vinegar is made from beer, while red and white wine vinegars are made as their names would suggest. Vinegar is generally the enemy of wine, and too much vinegar in cooking or in a salad dressing, for instance, can spoil the flavour of any delicate wine that is served with it, but wine vinegars are much less dangerous in this respect than is malt vinegar. Very often necessary sourness can be given to a dish or salad by the use of lemon juice instead of vinegar when wine is going to be served.

VINHO VERDE   See PORTUGUESE TABLE WINES.

VINICULTURE   The growing of grapes.

VIN JAUNE   See FRANCE, THE LESSER KNOWN WINES.

VINO SANTO   See ITALIAN WINES.

VINS DE GARDE   See FRANCE, THE LESSER KNOWN WINES.

VINTAGES   The vintage is the gathering of the grapes, and hence a wine sold with a specific vintage year is (or should be) made exclusively from grapes gathered in that year, though this is not an invariable rule and in some districts – Champagne for instance – a small admixture with wine of other years is permitted in order to compensate for the deficiencies that may exist in the wines of any year, however great. For instance, too much sunshine can produce a very big wine but one lacking in acid, and this could be compensated by the addition of a little wine from perhaps the previous year where sunshine was lacking and acid excessive. The vintage of a table wine is generally of great importance in assessing its quality and its maturity, but vintage charts and such like guides should be used with extreme caution. The first thing to remember is that wines of very great vintage years tend to take a long time to mature. 1945 clarets, for instance, although they look as if they will last for many decades, are only just coming into their own after twenty-eight years. 1961 is likewise an excellent vintage, but after twelve years few of the wines are showing anything like their full potential, and the less magnificent wines of 1962 are generally better to drink. The wines of poor vintage years, like the 1958 clarets, although never particularly good, are useful in that they mature quickly. The second thing to remember is that in any vintage year, whether it be outstandingly bad or outstandingly good, there are always a considerable number of exceptions to the general rule, and it is a connoisseur's delight to find them. A small pocket of land, for

Year	Claret	Red Burgundy	White Burgundy	Sauternes	Loire	Rhône	Rhine	Moselle	Champagne	Port
1945	7	5	—	6	—	7	—	—	4	7
1946	1	1	—	1	—	3	—	—	—	—
1947	5	4	—	6	4	6	—	—	4	6
1948	5	4	—	5	—	4	—	—	—	7
1949	6	5	—	6	—	7	—	—	4	—
1950	4	2	—	6	—	5	—	—	—	5
1951	0	0	—	1	—	2	—	—	5	—
1952	5	5	4	5	—	6	6	5	5	—
1953	5	4	3	5	—	6	1	1	—	5
1954	3	2	1	1	—	3	4	4	5	7
1955	5	4	3	7	—	6	—	1	—	—
1956	0	0	0	1	—	3	3	3	—	—
1957	4	5	4	4	—	6	3	3	6	5
1958	4	2	3	4	—	4	6	6	—	—
1959	6	6	4	6	—	6	1	2	6	7
1960	4	0	0	3	—	6	5	4	6	—
1961	7	6	5	7	—	7	3	3	—	—
1962	6	5	5	5	—	6	2	2	7	7
1963	1	1	1	0	—	2	6	6	—	—
1964	6	6	6	3	5	6	1	1	—	—
1965	1	0	1	0	—	2	6	5	—	7
1966	7	6	7	4	5	6	5	4	—	6
1967	6	4	6	5	6	6	3	2	—	—
1968	1	1	3	0	2	2	6	6	—	—
1969	5	7	7	6	7	5	5	4	—	—
1970	6	5	7	7	6	6	5	4	—	—

7 = the best   0 = no good

instance, may be devastated by hail or may be the only bit to miss being so devastated. Heavy rain at vintage time may fail to reach one end of a vineyard area, or an isolated vineyard may somehow catch all the sun that there is. Much, too, depends upon the amount of care and skill with which a grower makes his wine. In a bad year, a good wine may still be made in small quantities by very careful selection of grapes, while in a great year a thoroughly bad wine may be made by letting the fermentation get out of hand in the hot weather, so all generalizations about vintages need to be taken with a pinch of salt. Having said that, here is the vintage chart published by the International Wine and Food Society in 1972. Reproduced here with their permission, it is one of the most reliable general guides available.

VODKA A white spirit with very little flavour produced from potatoes or grain. It is the national drink of Russia and Poland where it is normally drunk neat and chilled. It is now finding favour in the west, and is often used as an ingredient of cocktails such as a vodkatini (a dry Martini made with vodka instead of gin), or a bloody Mary, consisting of three parts vodka to four parts of tomato juice and one part of lemon juice with a good dash of Worcester sauce. Although vodka in its natural form is practically flavourless, specially flavoured vodkas (comparable with the corresponding gins) are now becoming available.

VOLNAY See BURGUNDY.

VOSNE-ROMANÉE See BURGUNDY.

VOUGEOT See BURGUNDY.

VOUVRAY See LOIRE.

WACHENHEIM See RHINE.

WEEPER A bottle with a defective cork that lets the wine seep out. Such bottles should be drunk at once, or alternatively topped up to fill the ullage and then recorked. The latter course is only of use is the bottle is caught in time before the wine has gone bad.

WEHLEN See MOSELLE.

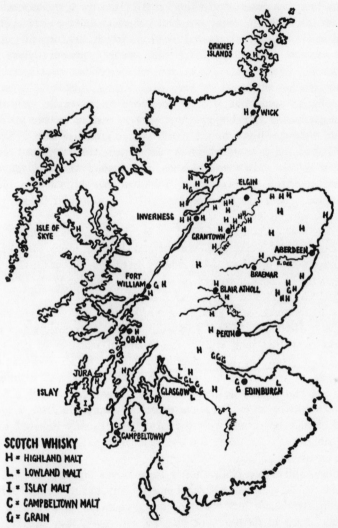

SCOTCH WHISKY
H = HIGHLAND MALT
L = LOWLAND MALT
I = ISLAY MALT
C = CAMPBELTOWN MALT
G = GRAIN

WHISK(E)Y Whisk(e)y has been defined in English law as being
a spirit obtained by distillation from a mash of cereal grains
saccharified by the diastase of malt. In simpler words it is the
spirit distilled from fermented grain, the initial product from
which it is distilled being something like beer. Whiskies are

produced in many countries, the flavour varying considerably from one to another, depending on the grain used, the techniques of the distiller, the local water, the method and time of ageing, and so on. Ageing is achieved by keeping the spirits in oak casks. For Scotch, sherry casks are used where possible, giving an additional flavour and also colour. Further colour may be added with caramel or traces of very dark sherry. Although whiskies do change somewhat if kept long enough in bottle – and not necessarily for the better – they do not mature in bottle. The most famous whisky in the world is undoubtedly Scotch. Spelling has varied over the years. A century ago, the recognized spelling of Scotch whisky was with an 'e', nowadays the 'e' is left out when referring to Scotch or Canadian but put in for other whiskies. These are (in alphabetical order) Bourbon (which *see*) Corn, Irish and Rye.

Scotch is of course distilled in Scotland and falls into three classes: malt, grain and commercial blends, these last being blends of the first two. Malt whisky is the classic spirit, distilled originally by small farmers mostly in the Highlands. It is made entirely from malted barley and is distilled in pot stills. There are four main areas, each producing whisky of a characteristic kind, namely Highland Malts, Lowland Malts, Campbeltowns, and Islays. A vatted malt whisky is a blend of whiskies of different ages but from the same distillery. These are all great spirits (though of course the quality varies from distillery to distillery) and are real whisky drinkers' whiskies, taken neat or with a little water – nothing else. They are especially enjoyable after a meal and should be drunk with the care more usually devoted to a liqueur brandy, including the use of a good glass of a shape that lets the aroma collect.

Grain spirits are made mostly from barley and are distilled in patent (Coffey) stills. Although not by any means neutral white spirits, they have little of the whisky character and tend to be rather sharp in flavour. But blended with malt, they provide all the popular Scotch whiskies of commerce, taking their style from the malts but providing a spirit which is less powerfully flavoured and easier to knock back. The method of blending is a closely guarded secret, as is the proportion of malt to grain. It is probably fairly safe to say, though, that commercial whiskies contain about 40 per cent malt to 60 of grain, and may well include 40 or so different spirits chosen to produce a blend of precisely the style required – a highly skilled job. All Scotch has by law to be matured for at least three years in the wood. Most is matured for longer.

Canadian whiskey is distilled in Canada from a mash of corn (maize), rye and barley, using patent stills and matured in wood. It is generally smooth and light with a flavour that is all its own.

Corn whisky is distilled in the United States in patent stills from a mash containing not less than 80 per cent corn. It is seldom aged and hence generally very rough and raw.

Irish whiskey is distilled mostly from malted barley in pot stills. The malting is done in a different way, though, and this helps in providing a flavour that is distinctly different from Scotch. It is also distilled three times as compared with twice in Scotland. Although at the moment much more Scotch is sold, Irish whiskies are very good indeed. A century or so ago Irish whiskey was at least as important commercially as Scotch and the rise of the latter can be attributed at least as much to the business acumen of the Scots as to the flavour.

Rye whiskey distilled in the United States in patent stills from a mash contining not less than 51 per cent rye.

WILTENGEN See MOSELLE.

WINE The suitably fermented juice of freshly gathered ripe grapes. But see also COUNTRY WINES and BRITISH WINES.

WINKEL See RHINE.

WOODY A taste of wood acquired when a beverage has been too long in cask.

XÉRÈS French for sherry.

YQUEM See BORDEAUX, WHITE.

YUGOSLAVIA Yugoslavia provides good quality wines at very reasonable prices. The most important wine growing province in terms of quality (though it only accounts for some 9 per cent of the total production) is Slovenia, which includes the well-known area of Ljutomer, more usually spelt, in English speaking countries, Lutomer. Most of the wines are sold under the varietal names of the vines producing them: Riesling, Sylvaner, Traminer,

Sauvingnon and the indigenous Sipon, a variety of Furmint. The Riesling is the most popular, but perhaps too popular as Yugoslav Rieslings hardly taste characteristic of the Riesling grape and tend to be over sulphured. The Traminers and even the Sylvaners tend to be better. There is also a sweet wine sold under the name of Tigermilk, vinified from Ranina grapes in Tadgona.

Zell   See Rhine.

Zeltingen   See Moselle.

Zwicker   See Alsace.